Beautiful wire jewelry for beaders 2

Beautiful wire jewelry 2 for beaders

Wire, beads, metal, & more!

Irina Miech

KALMBACH BOOKS

Kalmbach Books
21027 Crossroads Circle
Waukesha, Wisconsin 53186
www.Kalmbach.com/Books

Photography © 2010 Kalmbach Books

Published in 2010
14 13 12 11 10   1 2 3 4 5

Manufactured in the United States
of America

Publisher's Cataloging-in-Publication Data

Miech, Irina.
   Beautiful wire jewelry for beaders. 2 /
Irina Miech.

     p. : col. ill. ; cm.

   "Wire, beads, metal and more."
   ISBN: 978-0-87116-418-6

   1. Jewelry making—Handbooks,
manuals, etc. 2. Wire jewelry—Handbooks,
manuals, etc. 3. Wire jewelry—Patterns.
4. Beadwork—Handbooks, manuals, etc.
5. Beadwork—Patterns. I. Title.

TT212 .M54345 2010
739.27

CONTENTS

INTRODUCTION

I love the adaptable nature of wire. Whether you want to bring forth a simple, clean look or the organic, natural designs I adore, you can achieve it with wire.

Wire is a graceful backdrop to the many shapes, sizes, colors, and textures of beads. I rarely shape a piece of wire jewelry that isn't enhanced by a bead or two—or many, many more. The two materials complement each other beautifully, and I explore this wonderful relationship throughout the jewelry projects featured in these pages.

Readers of my first wirework book will notice that I cover some new creative territory in these designs. You'll see applications of fundamental wireworking skills alongside new techniques such as doming, riveting, and stamping. I've incorporated metal blanks in some projects, and I've added color and depth by using copper and brass in addition to my versatile workhorse wire, sterling silver.

Wireworkers who appreciate a touch of Victorian elegance will be pleased to see several projects that use antiqued brass filigree findings. These surprisingly adaptable components can be molded into a variety of forms or used as a base for attaching other elements.

As you make the projects, you'll discover new ways of adding embellishment, texture, and layers to wirework. Whether you're just starting your wire journey or have some years of experience, I hope you'll find many projects that stir your imagination and build your skills.

Irina Miech

How to use this book

This book features projects in a variety of styles that I designed as a thorough introduction to working with wire. If you are new to these techniques, work through the projects in the order they appear to build a fine set of skills. If you're more experienced, choose any project you like and let the step-by-step instructions and photos guide you through.

The projects use many basic wire skills, such as making loops and shaping spirals, and introduce a few easy metalworking techniques that will bring a new look to your wire jewelry. Check the tab on the right-hand side of each page to see what you'll learn in each project. This color-coded tab also serves as a guide to identify which project section you're in—beginner (blue), intermediate (yellow-green), or advanced (reddish-tan).The first time a technique is used, the instructions explain it in detail. Refer back to this explanation as needed.

You'll find a summary of materials, tools, and basic techniques in the back of the book, starting on p. 100. If you're entirely new to wireworking, you may want to read this section first. Those who have some experience with wire can scan this section for a refresher on the basic skills and my approach to wirework: working from the wire coil, making basic and wrapped loops, adding patina with liver of sulfur, and other information.

The wire used in the projects is round wire unless specified in the materials list as a different shape, such as half-round or rectangular.

With each project you'll see photos of several design options to jump-start your creative thinking. Combine techniques and improvise on the look to create your own variations.

SPECIALTY TOOLS

Your tools will become an extension of your hands as you shape wire into beautiful jewelry. Buy the best you can afford—quality tools will last longer and be a pleasure to use.

As I began to incorporate more metalworking techniques into my wirework designs, I added some specialty tools to my kit. This page introduces those new tools; read more about my basic set of wireworking tools starting on p. 102.

A **two-hole screw punch** makes holes in soft metal as the screw is turned. The larger screw (typically black) pierces a ³⁄₃₂-in. (2.3 mm) hole that's perfect for riveting; the silver screw makes a ¹⁄₁₆-in. (1.6 mm) hole.

A **brass-head hammer** is a heavy hammer used with decorative or letter punches. You'll find these in one- and two-pound weights; I prefer the heavier hammer because it makes deep impressions.

The head of the **riveting hammer** has a flat side for making tube rivets and a tapered side for making solid rivets. In this book, I use the flat side to make rivets out of double-walled crimp tubes.

Each project lists the tools and materials you'll need. For more about other tools, types of wire, and findings used throughout the book, see p. 100.

Hole-punching pliers are best used on soft sheet metal such as copper or silver. They are easy to use on domed shapes and make slightly smaller holes than the screw punch (usually 1.25, 1.5, or 1.8 mm).

A large **metal file** is handy for smoothing wire ends for pins and the corners of rectangular wire.

A **center punch** is used for riveting. I use it with double-walled crimp tubes and a riveting hammer.

Texture hammers add surface interest to metal. They're available in a variety of patterns, including stripes, dots, diamonds, and others.

A metal **dapping block** is used with a metal dapping punch to dome metal blanks. Place the blank in a concave depression, hold the punch over the blank, and tap the punch with a brass-head hammer.

Letter and decorative punches come in a variety of designs, various alphabet fonts, and numbers. They're used with a brass-head hammer.

dapping block and punches

letter punches

two-hole screw punch

brass-head hammer

riveting hammer

decorative punches

hole-punching pliers

metal file

center punch

texture hammers

Colorful Gemstones

An easy way to start making wire jewelry is to use eyepins and headpins as ready-made connectors. In this project, you'll learn how to make a basic loop over a bead—a fundamental wire-shaping technique.

You'll need

Materials

18 in. (46 cm) ball chain

10–12 in. (25–31 cm) link chain

29 1½-in. (38 mm) eyepins

2 1½-in. headpins

2 earwires

22 ball-chain loop findings

31 assorted gemstone beads and pearls, approximately 10–20 mm

Tools and supplies

Chainnose pliers

Roundnose pliers

Side cutters

The chain and wire components used in this project are all base metal that is finished in a color called gunmetal. I suggest using gunmetal-color headpins and eyepins because they hold their shape better than the commonly available wire in that finish.

TO MAKE THE NECKLACE

1 Cut the ball chain into nine 2-in. (51 mm) segments. Attach a ball-chain loop finding to both ends of a chain segment and squeeze it with chainnose pliers. Repeat for all segments.

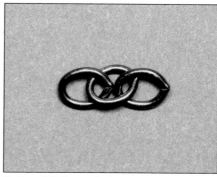

2 Cut 18 three-link segments of the link chain.

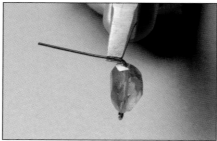

3 Make a basic loop above a bead: String a bead on an eyepin. Use flatnose pliers or your fingers to make a right-angle bend over the bead.

4 With the flat side of the side cutters toward the bead, trim the wire to ⅜ in. (10 mm).

5 Grasp the wire end with roundnose pliers and roll in the opposite direction of the bend to make a loop.

6 When you can't comfortably continue rolling, adjust the grasp of the pliers in the loop and continue rolling to form a complete circle of wire.

7 To connect the bead unit to the end of one of the three-link chain segments, open the loop slightly by moving the wire end toward you with chainnose pliers, add the chain, and close the loop.

8 Continue to link beads and chain in this way until you have a set of three beads connected by two segments of link chain.

9 Repeat step 8 until you have nine sets of three beads with chain in between.

10 Link each side of a bead-and-chain set to the loop at the end of a ball-chain component. Link segments in this way until the necklace is complete.

Use ball chain and crystals to make a faux lariat.

TO MAKE THE EARRINGS

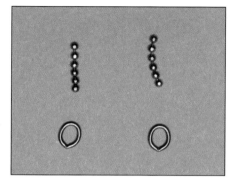

1 Cut two ½-in. (13 mm) segments of ball chain and two single chain links.

2 Attach a ball-chain loop finding to both ends of the ball chain and squeeze it with chainnose pliers.

3 String a bead on a headpin and connect it to the chain link with a basic loop.

4 Connect an eyepin to the chain link, string a bead, and make a basic loop that attaches to one end of the ball-chain loop. Attach the other end of the ball chain to the earwire.

5 Make a second earring.

Brass findings and gunmetal ball chain mix beautifully with crystals in this bracelet.

Ocean Surf

Wrapped loops are fundamental to wireworking. They are a secure way of connecting fine-gauge wire or headpins, and the even coil of wire that signifies a well-made wrap is an excellent design element. Perfect your technique while making this set—you'll start by making 35 wrapped-loop components for the necklace.

You'll need

Materials
45 1½-in. (38 mm) 24-gauge headpins
20–24 in. (51–61 cm) large-and-small link chain
47 5 mm jump rings
2 earwires
45 4–5 mm pearls
Hook clasp
Carved shell pendant

Tools and supplies
Chainnose pliers
Roundnose pliers
Side cutters

TO MAKE THE NECKLACE

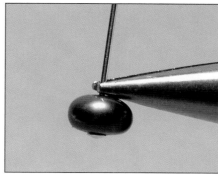

1 Make a wrapped loop above a bead: String a pearl on a headpin and grasp the wire above the pearl with the tip of the chainnose pliers.

2 Use your fingers to bend the wire over the pliers at a 90° angle.

3 Place the roundnose pliers just past the bend. Wrap the wire over the top jaw as far as it will go. Rotate the pliers in the loop and continue wrapping until you have a full circle.

4 You can center the loop over the bead by turning the pliers slightly while holding the bead. When the loop is centered, the wire should cross itself at a 90° angle.

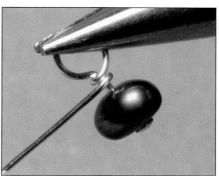

5 Holding the loop with chainnose pliers, use your fingers or a second set of pliers to wrap the wire into the gap between the loop and the bead. Make 2–3 wraps.

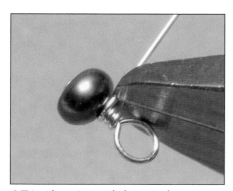

6 Trim the wire end close to the wraps.

7 Use chainnose pliers to tuck the wire end tightly between the wraps and the bead. Make a total of 35 wrapped-loop components.

8 Use two pairs of pliers to open a jump ring; open it wider than usual so you can easily slide on the pendant.

One way of ensuring uniform loops is by making a mark on your roundnose pliers with a permanent marker, then working at the same point each time. Another way is to shape your loops on one of the steps of forming pliers.

9 Cut a length of chain that has 20 large links, and put it aside for the earrings. Find the midpoint of the remaining chain. Connect the pendant to a link 1 in. (26 mm) from that point.

10 Using jump rings, connect 17 wrapped-loop components to the large links on each side of the pendant.

11 Connect the clasp to the short end of the chain using a jump ring.

12 Connect the last wrapped-loop component to the long end of the chain using a jump ring. (This end will serve as an extender.)

TO MAKE THE EARRINGS

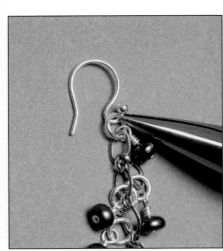

1 Make 10 wrapped-loop pearl components. Cut the reserved chain in half and attach five components to each segment of the chain using jump rings.

2 Attach one end of each chain component to an earwire.

Wrapped loops turn bead caps into flower charms in this bracelet.

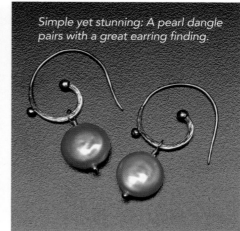

Simple yet stunning: A pearl dangle pairs with a great earring finding.

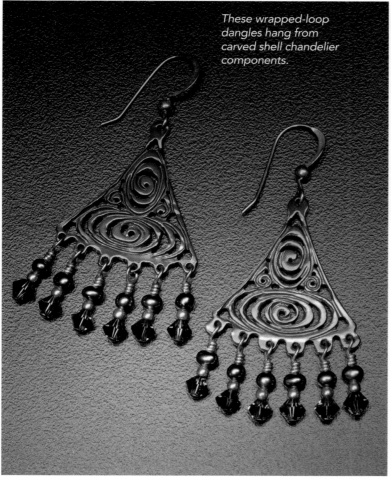

These wrapped-loop dangles hang from carved shell chandelier components.

bracelet

Elegant Citrine

After you have mastered making wrapped loops using headpins, progress to making them with wire for even more possibilities in your designs. In this project, you'll use wire to create the gemstone components that are focal points in this elegant bracelet.

You'll need

Materials

15 in. (38 cm) 22-gauge half-hard sterling
   silver wire
5 gemstone beads, approximately 10 x 15 mm
22 6 mm sterling silver jump rings
6 8.5 mm twisted sterling silver jump rings
Toggle clasp

Tools and supplies

Chainnose pliers
Roundnose pliers
Side cutters
Liver of sulfur

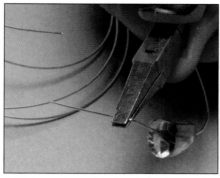

1 String a bead onto the wire and slide it down. Make a 90° bend about 1 in. (26 mm) from the end of the wire.

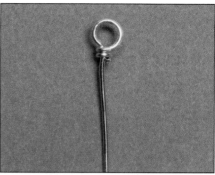

2 Working just above the bend, make a wrapped loop. Use chainnose pliers to hold the loop while you make two wraps below the loop. Trim the excess wire and tuck in the wire end.

3 Slide the bead to the loop. Hold the wire with the tip of the chainnose pliers above the bead and make a 90° bend.

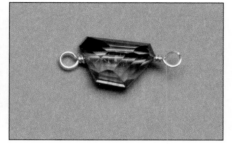

4 Make a wrapped loop on the other side of the bead.

Repeat steps 1–4 to create five gemstone components.

5 Connect a gemstone component to a twisted ring with a jump ring.

6 Add a second jump ring next to the first.

7 Repeat steps 5–6 to assemble the bracelet. After the gemstone components are linked, use a single jump ring on each end to attach the clasp.

8 Add patina with liver of sulfur.

It's safe to immerse hard gemstones such as quartz or onyx in liver of sulfur solution. If your project includes soft stones like turquoise or opal, which may discolor in the solution, you can add patina to the silver before starting to work with it. See p. 110 for more information about using liver of sulfur.

Mix it up! Linking a variety of sizes and textures of rings adds a great deal of interest to your jewelry. Using pairs of jump rings is a nice touch.

necklace and earrings

Spiral Harmony

Spiral imagery appears as a design motif in many cultures. In this project, the decorative spiral also serves a practical purpose as a headpin.

You'll need

Materials

25–30 in. (64–76 cm) 22-gauge half-hard
  sterling silver wire
12–15 in. (30–38 cm) 18-gauge dead-soft
  sterling silver wire
11 in. (28 cm) drawn cable sterling silver chain
14 mm silver disk component
Clay beads: 22 x 27 mm focal, 2 9 x 11 mms,
  12 5 x 6 mm rondelles
Hook clasp
2 earwires
1½-in. (38 mm) 24-gauge sterling silver
  headpin
2 2 mm sterling silver round beads
4 mm sterling silver jump ring

Clay beads by Clay River Designs

Tools and supplies

Chainnose pliers
Roundnose pliers
Flatnose pliers
Side cutters

*Create balance in an
asymmetrical design
by giving each side the
same visual weight. In
this necklace, a large
component on the left is
balanced by nine small
components on the right.*

TO MAKE THE NECKLACE

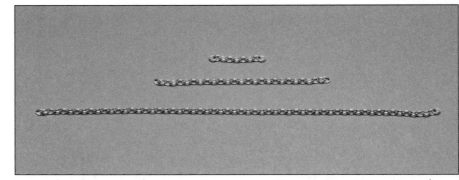

1 Cut the chain into three segments: 1 in. (26 mm), 3 in. (76 mm), and 7 in. (18 cm).

2 Using the 22-gauge wire, link nine rondelle beads into a chain by making wrapped loops. Leave the last loop on both ends unwrapped.

3 Link a rondelle to each side of the disc component with wrapped loops. Leave the outside loops unwrapped.

4 Connect the necklace by slipping the chain into the open loops and wrapping the loops. Connect the components in this order: 3-in. chain segment, chain of nine rondelles, 1-in. chain segment, rondelle-disk-rondelle component, 7-in. chain segment.

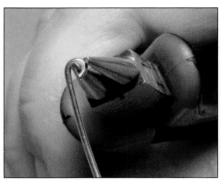

5 Using the 18-gauge wire, work at the tip of the roundnose pliers to make a tiny loop at the end of the wire.

6 If the start of the loop is not curved, trim the end with cutters.

7 Squeeze the sides of the loop with chainnose pliers to make the loop smaller.

8 Continue shaping the wire with chainnose pliers to form a second loop around the first.

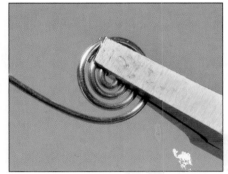

9 With flatnose pliers, grasp the spiral while bending the wire around with your fingers. Loosen your grip, regrip the spiral, and continue shaping until e spiral is about 7/16 in. (11 mm).

10 Use flatnose pliers to bend the wire at the base of the spiral to a 90° angle.

11 String the focal bead on the wire and bend the spiral upward in front of the bead. Trim the excess wire, leaving enough for a basic loop (3/8 in./10 mm).

12 Make a loop above the bead and attach the pendant to the end loop of the nine-rondelle chain.

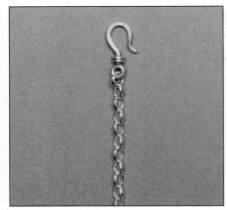

13 Use a jump ring to attach a hook clasp to the short side of the necklace.

14 On a headpin, string a 2 mm round bead, a clay rondelle, and another 2 mm round bead. Attach to the chain with a wrapped loop. This long end will serve as an extender chain.

TO MAKE THE EARRINGS

1 Cut two pieces of 18-gauge wire, each 2–3 in. (51–76 mm) long.

2 Follow steps 5–9 of the necklace instructions to make a small spiral at the end of each of the wires. Position them so they are mirror images of each other.

3 Use flatnose pliers to bend the wire at the base of each spiral to a 90° angle.

4 String a bead onto each wire and bend each spiral upward in front of the bead. Make basic loops above each bead and attach the components to earwires.

Scale, repetition,
and balance all
come into play in
an asymmetrical
necklace design.

A spiral headpin
and a carved bead
make a whimsical
charm.

Treasure Key

Skeleton keys have an aura of mystery about them. To whom did they belong? What did they unlock? Using them in your designs creates a vintage mood and expresses a connection to the past.

You'll need

Materials

12–15 in. (31–38 cm) 24-gauge bronze-color wire

Skeleton key

50 assorted beads, 3–4 mm (gemstones, pearls, crystals)

45–100 size 13 Charlotte seed beads

1½-in. (38 mm) 24-gauge sterling silver headpin

4 mm copper daisy spacer

8 mm sterling silver bead cap

Tools and supplies

Chainnose pliers

Roundnose pliers

Side cutters

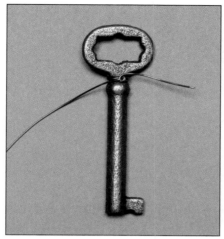

1 Starting about 3 in. (76 mm) from one end, lightly coil the wire around the top of the key two to three times. Wrap the short end around the long end to secure the coil.

2 String beads randomly on the long wire end, interspersing the Charlottes. Wrap the beaded wire tightly around the key, making sure there are no gaps between beads.

3 Tightly coil the end of the wire around the bottom of the key two to three times. Wrap the wire around itself again to secure it.

4 Trim each wire end to about 1 in. (26 mm) and make small spirals on both ends. Position the spirals so they hide the wrapped ends.

5 String a crystal, a daisy spacer, and a bead cap onto a headpin. Use a wrapped loop to attach the dangle to the coiled beaded wire.

Use Renaissance wax, a microcrystalline wax used in historic preservation, to maintain the patina of a skeleton key and other oxidized metals.

Because of their varied shapes and sizes, skeleton keys are excellent for creating layered looks.

Nouveau Vintage

Brass filigree components are malleable, so it's easy to shape them for many uses. In this project, a brass component transforms into a bail. The semiprecious stone donut adds color and substance that show the metal at its best.

You'll need

Materials

2 in. (51 mm) semiprecious stone donut

1⅛ x 1⅜ in. (29 x 35 mm) dragonfly stamping

1⅛ x 2⅜ in. (29 x 60 mm) brass filigree
   stampings

5 8 mm round brass filigree beads

3 8 x 12 mm oval brass filigree beads

8 4 x 6 crystal rondelles

13 4 mm brass jump rings

5 10 mm twisted brass jump rings

Brass lobster claw

2 1½-in. (38 mm) brass headpins

14 1½-in. brass eyepins

11 in. (28 mm) brass chain

2 in. (51 mm) brass extender chain

Tools and supplies

Chainnose pliers

Flatnose pliers

Roundnose pliers

Side cutters

1 Use flatnose pliers to curve the two filigree components to match the curve of the donut.

2 Connect the two filigree components on one side using three 4 mm jump rings.

3 Add two more rows of 4 mm jump rings.

4 Attach a twisted jump ring through the three end rings.

5 String a crystal onto a headpin and make a basic loop.

6 Attach the crystal dangle to the center 4 mm jump ring.

7 Use a 4 mm jump ring to attach the dragonfly stamping to the twisted jump ring.

8 Cut the chain into segments:
- two 1-in. (26 mm) segments
- six ½-in. (13 mm) segments
- one 2-in. (51 mm) segment
- one 3-in. (76 mm) segment

9 Put the unembellished side of the curved filigree component through the hole in the donut. Connect the two filigree components at the top with 4 mm jump rings. At the same time, add a 1-in. segment of chain to each ring.

10 On one side of the necklace, connect components in this pattern to the 1-in. chain: twisted jump ring, ½-in. chain, filigree bead on an eyepin, ½-in. chain. Make three of these segments and add a twisted jump ring.

11 Attach the 2-in. chain segment to the end ring. Attach the lobster claw clasp to the end link of chain using a jump ring.

12 On the other end, connect a pattern of crystal rondelles and round filigree beads on eyepins until you have six crystals and five filigree beads.

13 Attach the 3-in. chain segment to this side, then attach the extender chain using one of the chain links (these chain links are not soldered). String a crystal rondelle on a headpin. Attach the dangle to the end of the extender chain with a basic loop.

When I make a necklace that has either a hook or a lobster claw clasp, I attach the clasp on the side of the wearer's dominant hand to make it easy for her to manipulate the clasp.

Make dainty bails for petite components in the same way.

Hammered Disks

Metals, shapes, and textures blend for a modern look in this set.
The layered components move freely.

You'll need

Materials

6–8 in. (15–20 cm) 18-gauge dead-soft sterling silver wire

Copper disk blank, 1-in. (26 mm) diameter

2 copper disk blanks, ¾-in. (19 mm) diameter

3 6 x 9 mm pearls

3 1½-in. (38 mm) sterling silver ball headpins

3 6 mm copper jump rings

2 4 mm sterling silver jump rings

4 in. (10 cm) antiqued sterling silver chain

Sterling silver bail

2 earwires

Tools and supplies

Chainnose pliers

Flatnose pliers

Roundnose pliers

Hole-punching pliers

Side cutters

Bench block

Chasing hammer

Liver of sulfur

TO MAKE THE PENDANT

1 Place the large disk on the bench block and texture it by striking it with the chasing hammer.

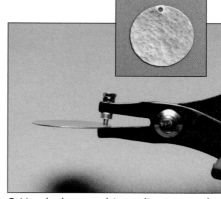

2 Use hole-punching pliers to make a hole about 2–3 mm from the edge of the disk. Add patina to the disks with liver of sulfur if desired.

3 Using about 2–3 in. (51–76 mm) of 18-gauge wire, create a spiral and end it with a hanging loop. Flatten and add some texture to the spiral with the chasing hammer.

4 String a pearl on a ball headpin. Attach the pearl dangle to a 1½-in. (38 mm) length of chain with a wrapped loop.

Try varying the shapes of the copper blanks or using a texture hammer in step 1.

5 Open a copper jump ring and attach the top loop of chain, the hammered disk, and the loop of the spiral.

6 Attach the bail and close the jump ring.

Dome the copper disks after texturing.

TO MAKE THE EARRINGS

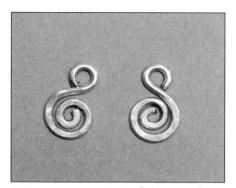

1 Repeat steps 1–5 of the pendant instructions for each earring using the small copper disks, 1½–2-in. (38–51 mm) lengths of wire for the spirals, and 1¼-in. (32 mm) segments of chain. Attach the spirals so they are mirror images of each other. Close the jump rings.

2 Attach the dangles to the earwires using silver jump rings.

An open silver component shows off the texture and patina of the disk beneath.

Eternity Knots

Although the intertwined knot is a classic element, the slight asymmetry of the design makes this necklace totally *au courant*.

You'll need

Materials

8–10 ft. (21.4–3 m) 18-gauge dead-soft
    sterling silver wire
1 in. (26 mm) half-round 16-gauge dead-soft
    sterling silver wire
2 ft. (61 cm) sterling silver chain
27 6–7 mm sterling silver jump rings
9 faceted 10 mm semiprecious stone beads
    with large holes
40 4 mm spacer beads
2 sterling silver earwires
2 sterling silver ball headpins

Tools and supplies

Chainnose pliers
Stepped forming pliers (5, 7, and 10 mm steps)
Roundnose pliers
Flatnose pliers
Side cutters

*Instead of using the
stepped forming
pliers to coil the wire,
you can use a metal
mandrel or a wood
dowel—any item with
a diameter of about
¼ in. (7 mm), which
equals a circumference
of about ⅞ in. (22 mm).*

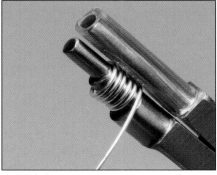

1 Coil the 18-gauge wire on the
center step of the forming pliers.

2 Cut the coiled wire into sections
of five coils each. Make 20 sections.

3 To make a knot, thread one
five-coil section onto another (as
you would thread a key onto a key
ring). Turn the two sections so all
wire ends are hidden inside.

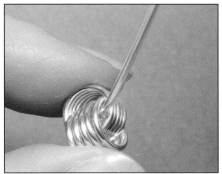

4 Squeeze the knot gently to
open a space and slide the knot
on one end of the remaining
18-gauge wire.

5 String a spacer on each side
of the knot and make a loop on
each end.

6 Repeat steps 3–5 to make a total
of 10 knot components.

7 String a bead with a spacer on
each side on the wire. Make a loop
on each end. Make a total of seven
bead components.

8 Use two jump rings to connect a knot component to each side of a bead component. Repeat to make five of these knot-bead-knot sections.

9 Cut four 2-in. (51 mm) lengths of chain and four 3-in. (76 mm) lengths of chain. Connect alternating lengths of chain to the end loops of each knot-and-bead section. Attach the remaining single bead components to each end. Add one of the remaining segments of chain to each end.

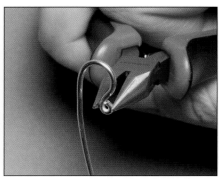

10 To make the clasp, bend 18-gauge wire into a hook shape around the center step of the forming pliers.

11 Using chainnose pliers, bend the tip of the wire into a tiny U shape.

12 Squeeze the U shape tight against the hook.

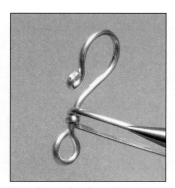

13 With flatnose pliers, grasp the wire below the hook and use your fingers to make a 90° bend below the pliers. Use roundnose pliers to make a basic loop below the bend.

14 Bend the half-round wire in half.

15 Place the bend around the neck between the hook and the loop. Coil the wire tightly around the stem several times. Trim and tuck the wire ends.

16 On one end of the necklace, slide the end link of chain into the loop of the clasp. Attach a jump ring to the other end.

TO MAKE THE EARRINGS

1 Make two bead components as in step 7 of the necklace. Attach two jump rings to the top loops of the bead components, then attach a single ring to the two rings of each component.

2 Attach the earwires to each single jump ring.

3 Cut two ⅜-in. (10 mm) lengths of chain. Slide the end link of each chain into the bottom loop of the bead components.

4 String two spacer beads on two ball headpins. Attach them to the end links of both chains with wrapped loops.

Make textured knots with twisted wire. For the single-knot pendant above, I wrapped twisted wire around thick-gauge round wire.

bracelet

Vintage Romance

The Victorian era was known for its ornate, opulent jewelry. In this modern interpretation of that popular look, elaborate filigree findings become settings for large, sparkling crystals.

You'll need

Materials
4 18 mm crystal rivolis
4 1⅜-in. (35 mm) 6-petal brass filigree
　　components
8 4 mm (small) brass jump rings
16 6 mm (medium) brass jump rings
5 10 mm (large) twisted brass jump rings
Brass filigree toggle bar
Brass filigree ring
Brass headpin
6 mm round crystal bead

Tools and supplies
Chainnose pliers
Flatnose pliers
Roundnose pliers
Side cutters

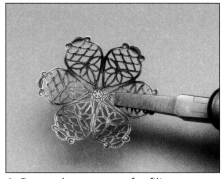

1 Grasp the center of a filigree component with flatnose pliers and flatten the entire piece. Then use flatnose pliers to bend the petals upward to give the component a slightly concave shape.

2 Using flatnose pliers, make a 90° bend in each petal as shown to make a setting.

3 Insert the rivoli into the setting and hold firmly while you bend the petals over the rivoli with your fingers. Work in pairs, bending facing petals at the same time. Tighten the petals against the rivoli using flatnose pliers.

4 Repeat steps 1–3 for the three remaining rivolis.

5 Slide a small jump ring through two adjacent openings on a point of each setting; repeat on the opposite side and for all four components.

 To put a new spin on a vintage design, use modern elements, such as textured jump rings.

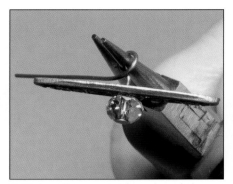

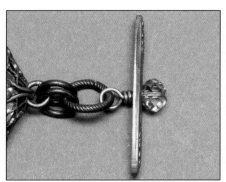

6 Attach two medium jump rings to each small jump ring. Use twisted jump rings to connect all four components.

7 String the crystal bead and the toggle bar onto a headpin and make a wrapped loop.

8 Attach the bar component to one end of the bracelet with a twisted jump ring.

9 Attach the filigree ring to the other end of the bracelet with a twisted jump ring.

Make quick-and-easy earrings with crystals.

Frame any undrilled crystal or cabochon. This pendant showcases a mabé pearl.

Free-form Wrapped Drusy

This versatile design can be adapted to a variety of stone shapes. Keep it simple and elegant or add whimsy with coils, spirals, and zigzags.

You'll need

Materials

33 in. (84 cm) 16-gauge half-round dead-soft
    sterling silver wire

Drusy cabochon, approximately ¾ x 1½ in.
    (1.9 x 3.8 cm)

2 6–7 mm sterling silver jump rings

Tools and supplies

Chainnose pliers

Stepped forming pliers (5, 7, and 10 mm steps)

Roundnose pliers

Flatnose pliers

Side cutters

Liver of sulfur (optional)

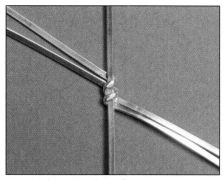

1 Cut the wire into four pieces: two 12 in. (31 cm), one 6 in. (15 cm), and one 3 in. (76 mm). With the round side of the wire facing out, wrap both 12-in. pieces around the 6-in. length, starting in the center of all three wires.

2 Wrap four to six times. Finish with the ends of the wrapping wires pointing in opposite directions.

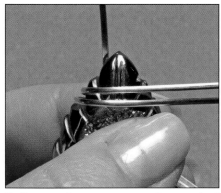

3 Center the stone over the vertical wire. Holding the stone firmly, wrap the top pair of wires from the side around the front of the stone as shown. Bring them to the back.

4 Remove the stone. Using chainnose pliers, tightly wrap the pair of wires once around the center back wire.

5 Reposition the stone in the top wraps. Bring the bottom pair of wires around to the front of the stone and then to the back in a similar way. Secure this pair by wrapping them around the center back wire.

Drusy refers to the layer of crystals, often quartz, that form on a host stone. The drusy I used has a thin coat of real gold bonded to a carved base stone.

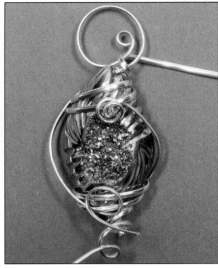

6 Bring one wire from each pair to the front and make loose spirals at the top and bottom of the stone as shown. Secure each spiral by wrapping the wire through one of the wire wraps from step 3 (top) and step 5 (bottom).

7 Use the remaining center wire above the stone to make a large, loose spiral as shown.

8 Secure the spiral by wrapping one of the wires from the back around it. Trim and tuck any excess wire left at the back of the stone.

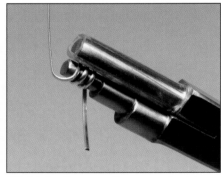

9 To make the bail, bend a 3-in. piece of wire into a U shape on the first step of the forming pliers.

10 Make three coils on each side of the U.

11 Use chainnose pliers to make a tiny loop on each end of the wire. Attach the bail to the pendant with two jump rings. Add patina with liver of sulfur if desired.

With free-form wrapping, you can make a setting for any shape of stone.

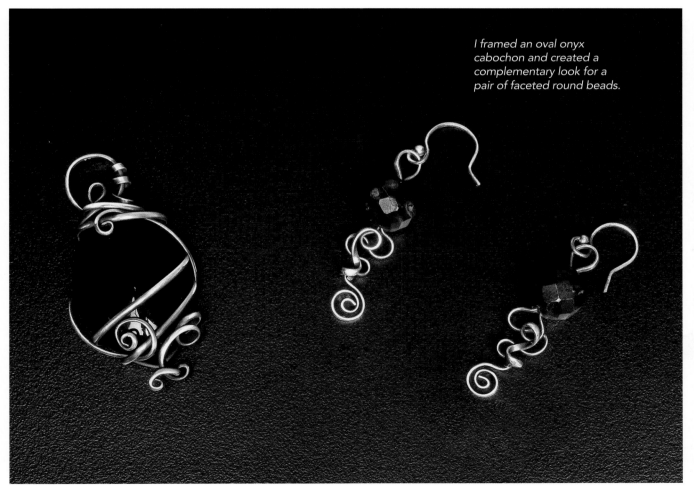

I framed an oval onyx cabochon and created a complementary look for a pair of faceted round beads.

Filigree Frame

A bit of wirework turns a filigree component into the perfect frame for a gemstone or pearl bead. Link an assortment of colorful framed beads into a charming bracelet.

You'll need

Materials
20 in. (51 cm) 24-gauge dead-soft sterling silver wire

10 assorted gemstone and pearl beads, 8–15 mm

10 filigree frame components

26 6 mm sterling silver jump rings

Toggle clasp

Tools and supplies
Chainnose pliers

Flatnose pliers

Side cutters

 Before you get started, pair each bead with a filigree frame, matching size and shape.

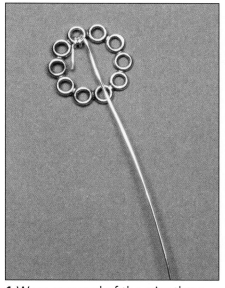

1 Wrap one end of the wire three times around one of the loops of a filigree component.

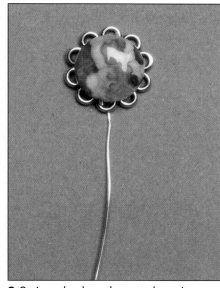

2 String the bead onto the wire and pass the wire down through a nearby loop.

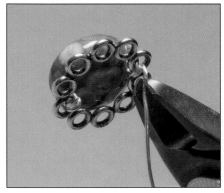

3 Wrap the wire three times around the loop. Trim the excess wire.

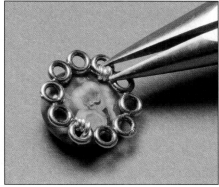

4 Tuck in both wire ends using chainnose pliers.

5 Repeat steps 1–4 to make a total of 10 framed components. Connect all of the components using jump rings.

6 Attach half of the clasp to each end with a chain of jump rings.

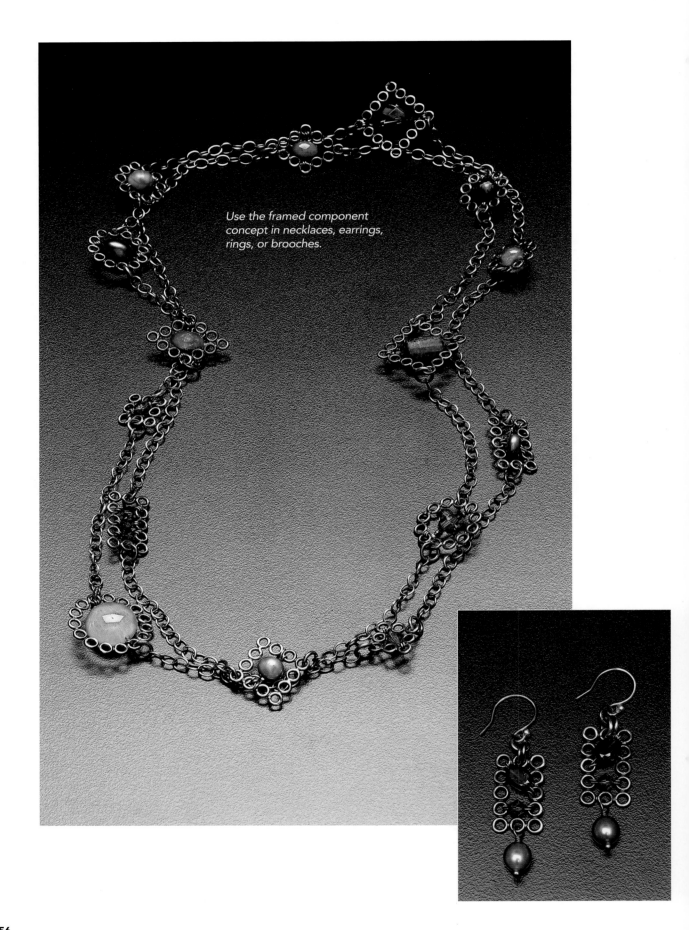

Use the framed component concept in necklaces, earrings, rings, or brooches.

Road to Hana

The town of Hana on the Hawaiian island of Maui is a remote, undeveloped paradise. Its gorgeous beaches, rugged coast, and picturesque highway full of switchbacks, waterfalls, and bridges make it one of my favorite places in the world. This bracelet is my tribute.

You'll need

Materials

36 in. (76 cm) 18-gauge dead-soft sterling
  silver wire
12 6–7 mm sterling silver jump rings
6 large-hole semiprecious stone beads:
  24 mm, 2 18 mm, 3 6–10 mm

Tools and supplies

Chainnose pliers
Roundnose pliers
Flatnose pliers
Side cutters
Texture hammer
Bench block
Liver of sulfur (optional)

1 Cut two 6-in. (15 cm) lengths of
wire and six 4-in. (10 cm) lengths.

2 Using one of the 4-in. lengths,
make a spiral at each end. Leave
about 1 in. (26 mm) between the
centers of the spirals.

3 Place the spiral component on
the bench block. Strike the surface
with a texture hammer until it has a
texture you like.

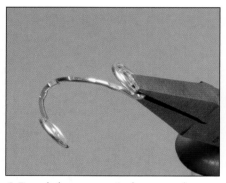

4 Bend the two spirals toward
one another as shown, with the
textured side facing out.

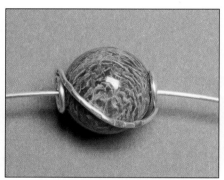

5 String the component and an
18 mm bead onto a 6-in. wire
so the bead is between the two
spiral caps.

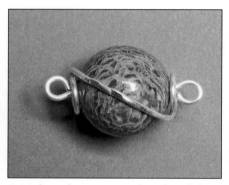

6 Make a loop on each side of the
component. Set the trimmed wire
aside for steps 7 and 12.

7 Repeat steps 2–6 to make a
second bead-and-wire component.

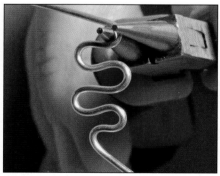

8 Using the 6-in. piece of wire,
make a soft zigzag with roundnose
pliers. Leave about 1½ in. (38 mm)
of straight wire on each side of
the zigzag.

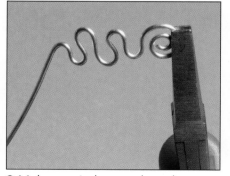

9 Make a spiral on each end.

10 Texture the zigzag component.

11 Bend the spirals toward each other as shown.

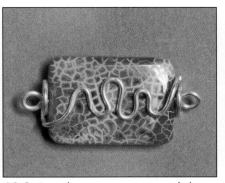

12 String the component and the 24 mm bead on the remaining reserved wire and make a loop at each end.

13 Make an open spiral at the end of a 4-in. piece of wire. Texture the spiral.

14 String a small bead on the wire and make a small open spiral on the other side of the bead. Working carefully so you don't damage the bead, texture the spiral. Make a second beaded component in a similar way, adding a zigzag if desired.

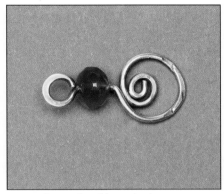

15 Make a third beaded component for the loop end of the clasp, making an open, textured spiral on one end and a flattened loop on the other.

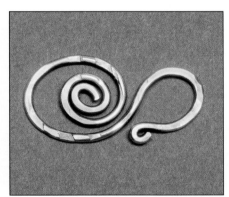

16 To create the hook component, make an open, textured spiral on one end of the remaining piece of wire and a hook at the other. Make a tiny U at the tip of the hook. Squeeze the U with chainnose pliers to tighten it against the hook. Slightly flatten the curve of the hook on the bench block.

17 Texture all of the jump rings. Connect the components into a bracelet using pairs of the textured jump rings. Add patina with liver of sulfur if desired.

When you use texture hammers, remember that the texture on the hammer is the reverse of what you'll see on the surface of your metal. Texture that is convex on the hammer will be concave and vice versa.

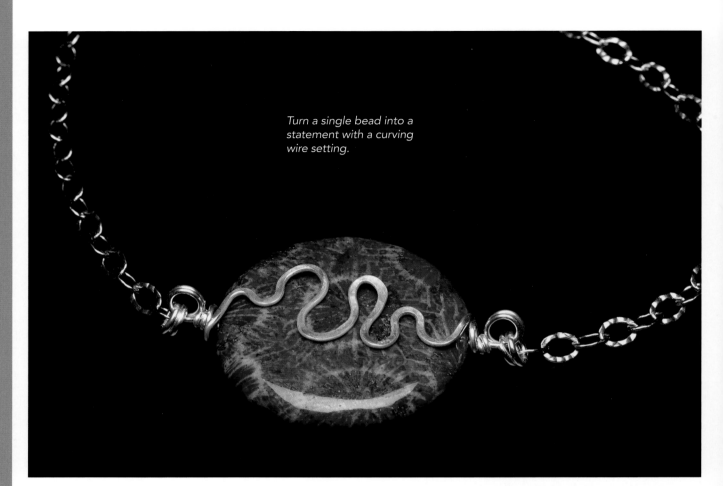

Turn a single bead into a statement with a curving wire setting.

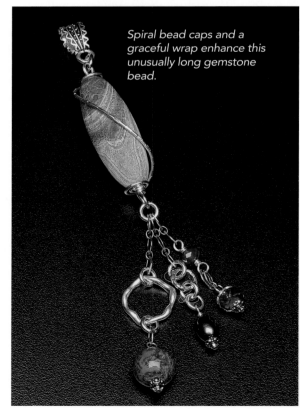

Spiral bead caps and a graceful wrap enhance this unusually long gemstone bead.

Spiral Cabochon Wrap

I enjoy finding new ways to showcase the beauty of natural gemstones.
In this project, the sparkle of the crystals complements the earthy appeal
of the cabochon.

Materials

12 in. (30 cm) 18-gauge dead-soft sterling
silver wire

12 in. 24-gauge dead-soft sterling silver wire

20 x 50 mm gemstone cabochon

12–15 2 mm round crystals

12–15 2 mm Thai silver cubes

Tools and supplies

Chainnose pliers

Flatnose pliers

Stepped forming pliers (5, 7, and 10 mm steps)

Side cutters

1 Working on the center step of the forming pliers, make a double loop in the center of the 18-gauge wire. This will be the bail.

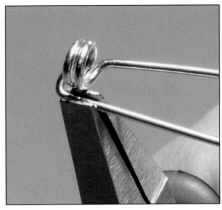

2 At the base of the bail, bend each wire using flatnose pliers so they are pointed in the same direction as shown.

3 Center the cabochon over the bail and wrap both ends of the wire tightly around the stone, curving downward. Try to keep the wire ends parallel but separate as they curve over the front of the stone.

4 Continue shaping the wire ends in a very loose spiral around the front and back of the stone as shown.

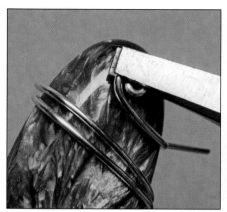

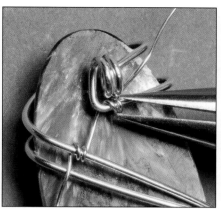

5 Make small spirals in the wire ends, one at the front and one at the back of the stone.

6 On the back, connect and reinforce the 18-gauge wire wrap using 24-gauge wire, tightening with chainnose pliers. Use short lengths as necessary.

For best results, choose a long, narrow cabochon. The length of this seraphinite cab allows room for a loose spiral, which is the foundation of this wrap.

7 Connect a piece of 24-gauge wire to the 18-gauge wire on the back of the stone with tight wraps near the edge. Bring the wire forward between the upper pair of wires. String beads on the 24-gauge wire, alternating crystals and silver cubes, until you reach the other side of the stone.

8 Wrap the wire securely around the 18-gauge wire on the back of the pendant.

9 Repeat steps 7–8 for the lower pair of wires.

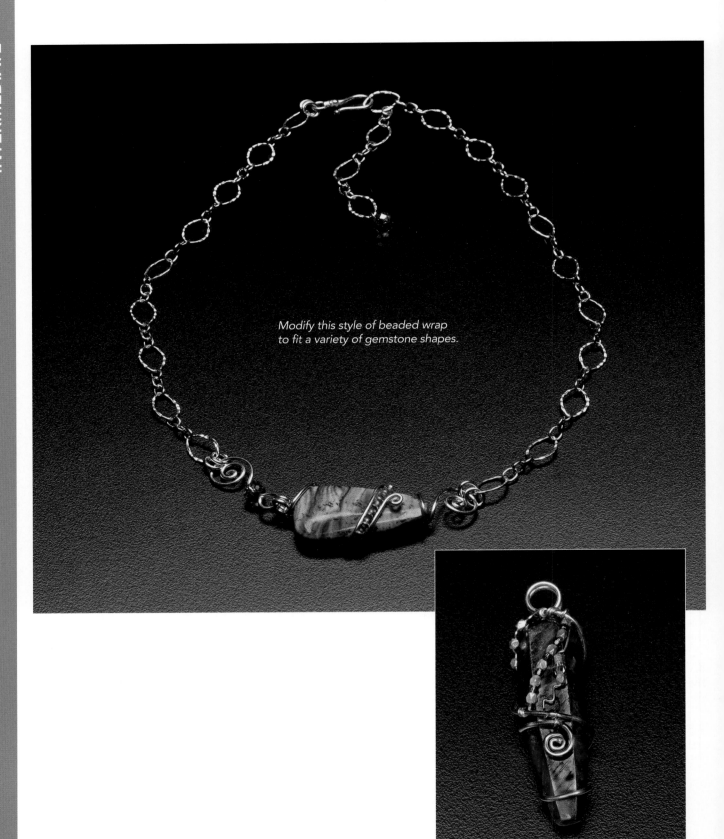

Modify this style of beaded wrap
to fit a variety of gemstone shapes.

Exotic Coins

Incorporating found objects into your jewelry adds character and personal charm. These earrings use donut-shaped brass coins paired with sterling silver findings to create a contemporary Bohemian feel.

You'll need

Materials

5–6 in. (13–15 cm) 18-gauge dead-soft sterling silver wire

3–4 in. (7.6–10 cm) 24-gauge dead-soft sterling silver wire

2 donut-shaped coins

4 2 mm double-walled crimp tubes

2 6–8 mm stone rondelle beads

2 4–5 mm brass beads

2 sterling silver earwires

2 4 mm sterling silver jump rings

2 6 mm copper jump rings

Tools and supplies

Chainnose pliers

Roundnose pliers

Side cutters

Riveting hammer

Bench block

Center punch

Cup bur

Chasing hammer

Fine-tip Sharpie marker

Two-hole screw punch

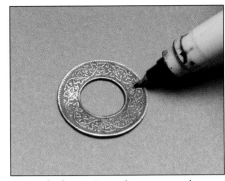

1 Mark the coins where you plan to pierce holes. Make two marks opposite each other approximately 2 mm from the edge.

2 Use the large side (black screw) of the punch to pierce the holes.

3 Place a crimp tube upright on the bench block. Position the center punch on top of the crimp tube.

4 Gently hammer the punch with the riveting hammer until one end of the tube is slightly flared.

Double-walled crimp tubes (three tubes on the left in the photo at right) make sturdy rivets. The metal is a tiny bit thicker than standard crimps (on the right).

5 Turn the crimp over. Place the coin on top of it so the tube is in one of the holes.

6 Use the punch and the riveting hammer to slightly flare the other end of the tube.

7 Use the riveting hammer to tap gently on both ends of the tube until it flattens into a rivet around the hole. Make a second rivet in the other hole.

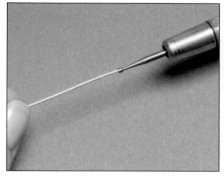

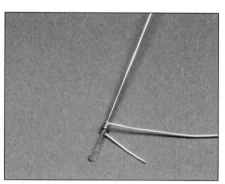

8 To make a paddle headpin, use a cup bur to smooth one end of a 2½-in. (64 mm) piece of 18-gauge wire.

9 Hammer the wire end flat with the chasing hammer.

10 Using 24-gauge wire, make three to five coils around the base of the paddle headpin.

Some coins are made out of a hard alloy that may stress your two-hole punch. If you're having trouble getting through the metal, you may want to choose a different coin.

11 String a rondelle bead. Wrap the 24-gauge wire loosely around the bead, moving in the same direction as the coils. Make three to five coils over the bead.

12 Make several coils spaced slightly apart and two tight coils. Trim the wire. Make a loop in the 18-gauge wire. Connect the paddle headpin component to the coin using a silver and a copper jump ring.

13 String a brass bead on 18-gauge wire and make a loop on each side. Attach it to the top of the coin and to the earwire.

14 Make a second earring.

With or without rivets, coins make intriguing links, charms, or focal points.

Butterfly Dreams

This project demonstrates how traditional metalworking techniques can be used to create one-of-a-kind components and centerpieces.

You'll need

Materials

1 x 1½ in. (2. 5 x 3.8 cm) 18-gauge rectangular copper blank

¾ x 1¼ in. (1.9 x 4.4 cm) brass butterfly stamping

3 6 mm copper jump rings

3 2 mm double-walled crimp tubes

2 3 mm double-walled crimp tubes

Brass flower charm

Tools and supplies

Chainnose pliers

Flatnose pliers

Screw-action punch

Bench block

Brass-head hammer

Decorative punches

Letter punches

Center punch

Fine-tip Sharpie marker

Pencil

Ruler

Liver of sulfur (optional)

1 Position the butterfly stamping on top of the blank and trace the outline with a pencil.

2 To texture the area outside of the traced line, place the metal blank on the bench block. Hold the decorative punch firmly over the blank and strike the punch with the brass-head hammer. Move the punch around as you strike to texture the area, keeping the bottom of the blank clear.

3 If you'd like to stamp your word in a straight line, use the pencil and a ruler to draw guidelines. You can also sketch the placement of the letters if you'd like.

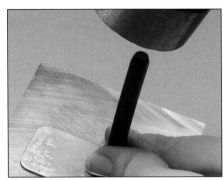

4 Use the letter punches and the brass-head hammer to imprint the letters one at a time.

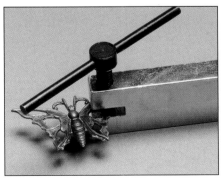

5 Use the large (black) side of the punch to pierce a hole on each side of the butterfly stamping.

6 Place the butterfly on the blank in the same position as before and trace the holes with the pencil.

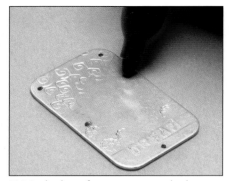

7 Mark dots for connector holes—two at the top and one centered at the bottom. Mark over the two pencil dots on the sides as well.

8 Use 2 mm crimp tubes to make rivets in the three connector holes.

 For a refresher lesson in riveting, see the Exotic Coins project on p. 65.

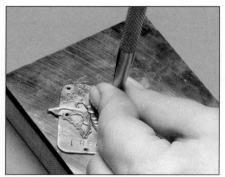

9 Use 3 mm crimp tubes to rivet the butterfly stamping to the copper blank.

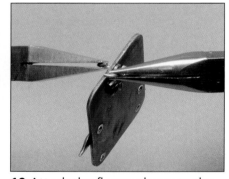

10 Attach the flower charm to the bottom of the pendant with a jump ring. Attach a jump ring to each of the top connector holes to create a bail.

11 Add patina with liver of sulfur if desired.

Need to place a hole with precision? Mark the spot, turn the punch over, slide the metal in, and look through the hole to center the mark as you turn the screw.

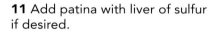

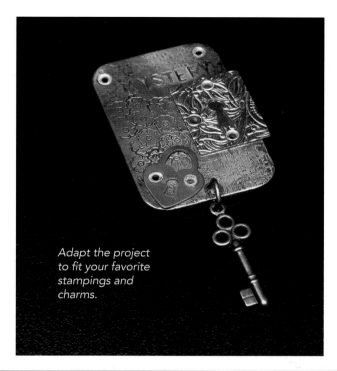

Adapt the project to fit your favorite stampings and charms.

A simple punched hole would have served here, but the silver rivets add a pleasing note of contrast.

Sea Glass

Over time, nature shapes each shard of sea glass into a unique piece of art. Use this wrapping technique to fashion a secure setting for any type of undrilled treasure.

You'll need

Materials

12–14 ft. (3.7–4.3 m) 24-gauge half-hard
   sterling silver wire

10–12 in. 22-gauge half-hard sterling
   silver wire

4 recycled glass beads, 8 x 12 mm

7 sea glass pieces, 15 x 20 mm to 20 x 29 mm

8 3 mm Thai silver cube beads

8 4–6 mm pearls

54 6 mm sterling silver jump rings

16 8.5 mm sterling silver twisted jump rings

Hook clasp

24-gauge sterling silver headpin

Tools and supplies

Chainnose pliers

Roundnose pliers

Side cutters

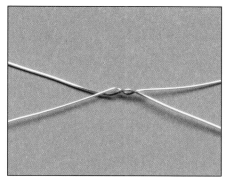

1 Cut the 24-gauge wire into 14 10–12 in. (25–30 cm) lengths. Twist two lengths of wire together two or three times starting in the center of each wire.

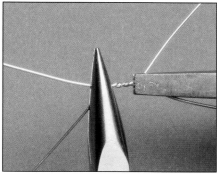

2 Holding one end of the twist steady with chainnose pliers, gently twist in the same direction with flatnose pliers to tighten.

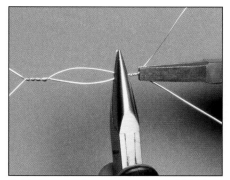

3 Make another twist about ¾ in. (19 mm) from the first. Tighten again using chainnose and flatnose pliers.

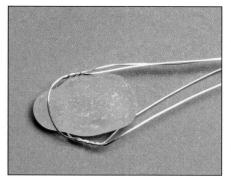

4 Insert a piece of sea glass into the loop formed between the twists. Bend the pairs of twisted wire along the sides of the glass.

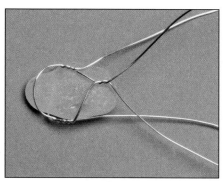

5 Twist one wire from each pair together as shown.

Not a collector of authentic sea glass? Faux sea glass that is made in a tumbler works just as well in this project.

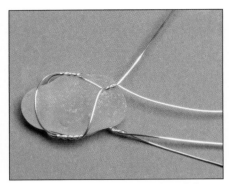

6 Repeat on the other side of the glass with the two remaining wires.

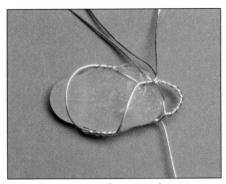

7 With one wire from each pair, make a twist about ⅜ in. (1.9 cm) long. Curve the twist to make a loop centered over the end of the glass. Secure the end of the twist by coiling both wires around the twist you made in step 5.

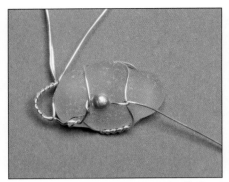

8 Use two wire ends to embellish and reinforce the wrapped setting. Space the wires out so they are nicely balanced, occasionally wrapping the working wire around the other wires.

9 Choose the side you'd like as the front, string a pearl onto a wire on that side, and secure the wire end by wrapping it around another wire.

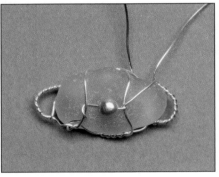

10 Use the two remaining wires to wrap in a free-form but balanced way, moving toward the other side of the glass and reinforcing with wraps and twists along the way. Use this pair of wires to make a second twisted loop at the other end of the glass. Trim the excess wire. Wrap and tuck the ends to conceal them.

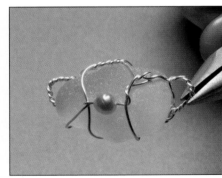

11 The glass will be oriented horizontally. Using chainnose pliers, adjust the loops to point slightly upward.

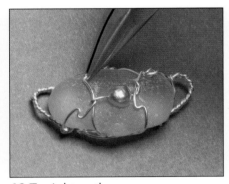

12 To tighten the wraps, grasp each segment of wire between wraps with the chainnose pliers and rotate the pliers to make a Z shape.

13 Repeat steps 1–12 to wrap the six remaining sea glass pieces.

14 On a 22-gauge wire, string a cube bead, recycled glass bead, and a cube bead, and make a wrapped loop at each end. Make a total of four wrapped-loop components.

15 Connect all of the wrapped glass pieces with links of two jump rings, a twisted ring, and two jump rings.

16 Add two wrapped-loop bead components to each end in the same way.

17 Create an extender chain by connecting jump rings, alternating a pair of jump rings with a twisted ring. Attach a wrapped-loop pearl headpin dangle to the end of the extender chain.

18 Attach a hook to the other end of the necklace with two jump rings.

19 Use liver of sulfur to add patina if desired.

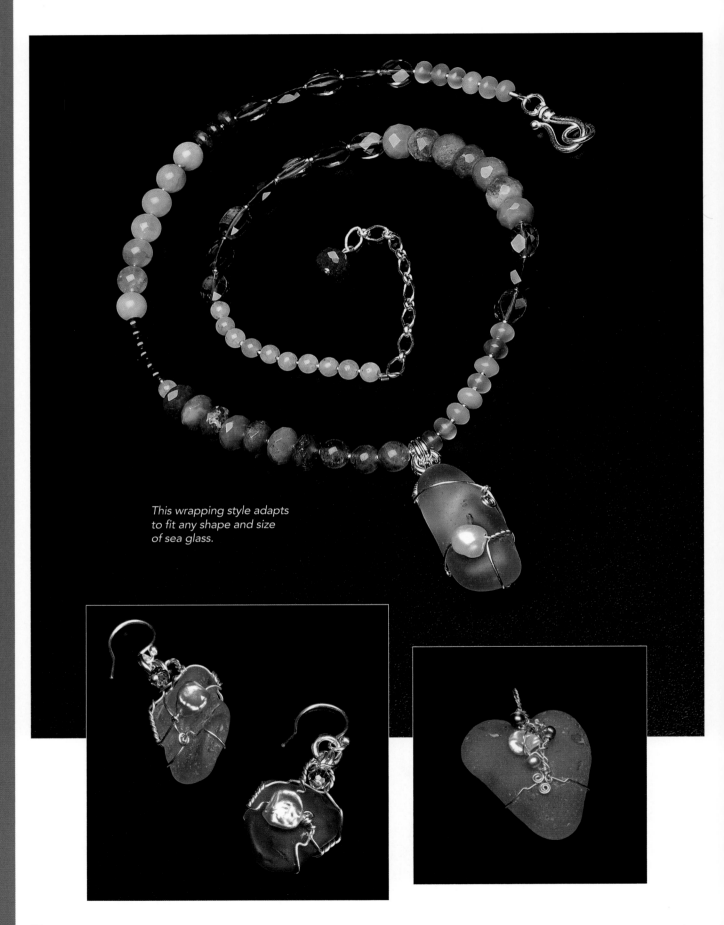

This wrapping style adapts
to fit any shape and size
of sea glass.

Cosmic Jewel

This wire-weaving technique is perfect for capturing undrilled crystals such as these rivolis. The geometric design perfectly frames the sparkling stone and gives it the timeless look of classic jewelry.

You'll need

Materials

31–38 in. (79–97 cm) 26-gauge dead-soft sterling silver wire

2 ⅞-in. (22 mm) 15-loop filigree components

2 ⅝-in. (16 mm) 10-loop filigree components

18 mm rivoli

2 12 mm rivolis

11 4 mm round crystals

1½ in. (38 mm) sterling silver rolo chain, 2 mm links

2 earwires

2 5–6 mm sterling silver jump rings

Tools and supplies

Chainnose pliers

Side cutters

TO MAKE THE PENDANT

1 Cut a 15–18-in. (38–46 cm) length of wire for the pendant and two 8–10-in. (20–25 cm) lengths for the earrings. Wrap the end of the long wire twice around loop 1 of a 15-loop filigree component.

2 Center the 18 mm rivoli over the filigree component. (At first you will have to hold the rivoli in place as you begin to create the setting.) Skipping three loops, pass the wire through loop 5 of the filigree component, front to back, so that it captures the edge of the rivoli.

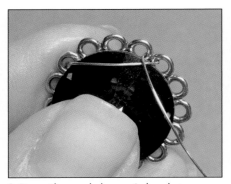

3 Pass through loop 4, back to front.

4 Continue to pass through every fourth loop in this way until you have gone all the way around the rivoli, creating a pentagon. At this point the rivoli should be secure.

5 Trim and tuck the starting end of the wire.

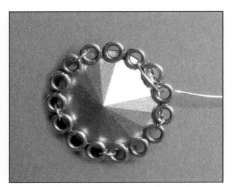

6 Pass the working wire from loop 2 to 15, passing the wire from the back to the front of the pendant.

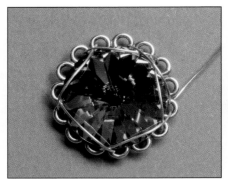

7 Skip three loops and pass the wire through loop 4, front to back.

8 Pass the wire through loop 3.

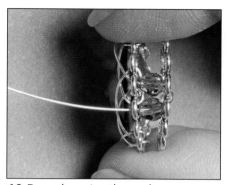

9 Pass through every fourth loop in this way until you have completed another pentagon. The wire end will be coming out of the back. String a crystal on the wire and pass the wire through a loop in the second filigree component.

10 Pass the wire through an adjacent loop, back to front, string a crystal, and pass through the first filigree component.

11 Continue weaving through the loops between both components in this way until you have strung eight crystals. The wire will be coming out of the front.

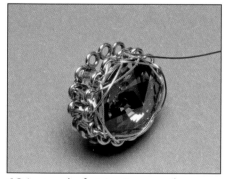

12 Instead of stringing another crystal, pass back through the next loop of the top filigree component, and back to the front through the next loop.

13 Add three crystals in the same way as before.

14 Repeat step 12, this time stringing the wire through the bottom filigree component to skip two loops. Secure the wire by wrapping it tightly around one of the loops and trim. Use chainnose pliers to tuck the end of the wire.

This pendant has no bail—it's designed to slide along a smooth chain or neckwire.

TO MAKE THE EARRINGS

1 Wrap the end of one of the short pieces of wire twice around loop 1 of a 10-loop filigree component.

2 Center the rivoli over the filigree component.

3 Skip two loops and pass the wire through loop 4 front to back, capturing the edge of the rivoli.

4 Pass the wire through loop 3 back to front.

5 Repeat, skipping two loops and passing down through every third loop and up the previous loop, until you have gone all the way around the rivoli.

6 Working from the back, pass the wire back to front from loop 2 to the center of the filigree component.

7 Pass the wire to the back between loops 2 and 3 and pass again through loop 2 back to front.

8 Skip two loops, and pass the wire back to front through loop 5 so that it captures the edge of the rivoli.

9 Pass the wire back to front through loop 4.

10 Repeat, skipping two loops and passing down through every third loop and up the previous loop, until you have completed another pentagon. The wire should exit the back.

11 Secure the wire by wrapping it tightly around one of the loops and trim. Use chainnose pliers to tuck the end of the wire.

12 Attach a rivoli component to half of the chain with a jump ring. On the other end of the chain, thread the last link onto an earwire.

13 Make a second earring.

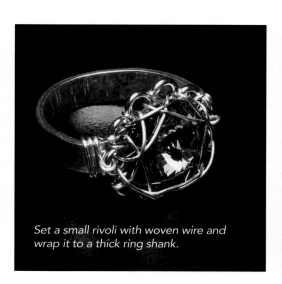

Set a small rivoli with woven wire and wrap it to a thick ring shank.

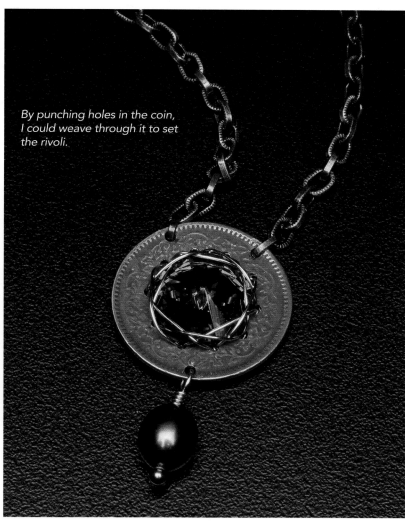

By punching holes in the coin, I could weave through it to set the rivoli.

Add jump rings to the Cosmic Jewel to make a bail.

pendant

Thailand Echoes

This pendant suggests the beauty and mystique of this country that lies in the heart of Southeast Asia. The focal bead has an elegant lotus motif, and tiny silver beads made by Thai Hill Tribes artisans are woven into a bead cap that is reminiscent of a ceremonial headdress.

You'll need

Materials

12 in. (30 cm) 18-gauge dead-soft sterling silver wire

50 in. (1.3 m) 24-gauge dead-soft sterling silver wire

Assorted seed beads (size 14 to 11)

Assorted 2–3 mm Thai silver beads

32 mm focal bead

Spacer bead

6 mm bead

Tools and supplies

Stepped forming pliers (5, 7, and 10 mm steps)

Chainnose pliers

Roundnose pliers

Flatnose pliers

Side cutters

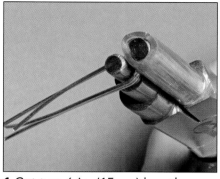

1 Cut two 6-in. (15 cm) lengths of 18-gauge wire. Center both wires on the first step of the stepped forming pliers and make a U-shaped bend.

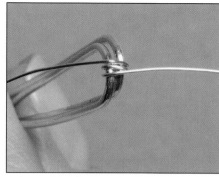

2 Starting about 5 in. (13 cm) from one end of the 24-gauge wire, bind the 18-gauge wires together in the center of the U bend with three or four wraps.

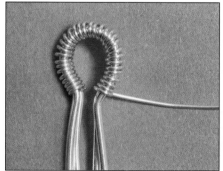

3 Using the smallest step of the forming pliers and flatnose pliers, shape the U into a hanging loop as shown. Wrap the entire loop with 24-gauge wire.

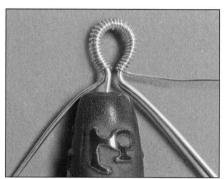

4 Trim the excess 24-gauge wire on the short side and tuck the end inside the loop. Bend three of the four wires coming out of the loop outward. Slide the focal bead onto the wire that is pointing down.

Choose accent beads that are smaller than 2 mm around (although their lengths can exceed 2 mm). Try for a variety of colors and textures.

5 Below the focal bead, string the silver spacer and the 6 mm bead. Make a small spiral below the 6 mm.

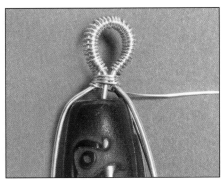

6 Use the long end of the 24-gauge wire to make three wraps around all three of the outside 18-gauge wires. On the next two or three passes, wrap once around each of the three wires.

7 As you reach the top of the bead, try wrapping three or more times around one of the wires to create an asymmetrical look.

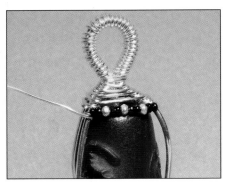

8 After a few passes, begin stringing beads on the working wire to fill the gaps between the 18-gauge wires. You may want to designate a front and back of the piece, and skip the step of adding beads to the back.

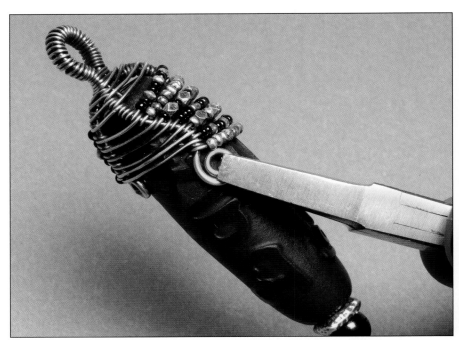

9 Use flatnose pliers to shape each 18-gauge wire into a pleasing curve as you continue beading the piece. When you're happy with the size and shape of the woven bead cap, wrap the 24-gauge wire a few times to secure, trim, and tuck the end. Trim the 18-gauge wires and end each with a spiral.

10 Add patina with liver of sulfur if desired.

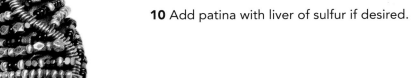

You can easily weave a cap to fit other shapes as well.

Weave a beaded wire bail for a gemstone donut.

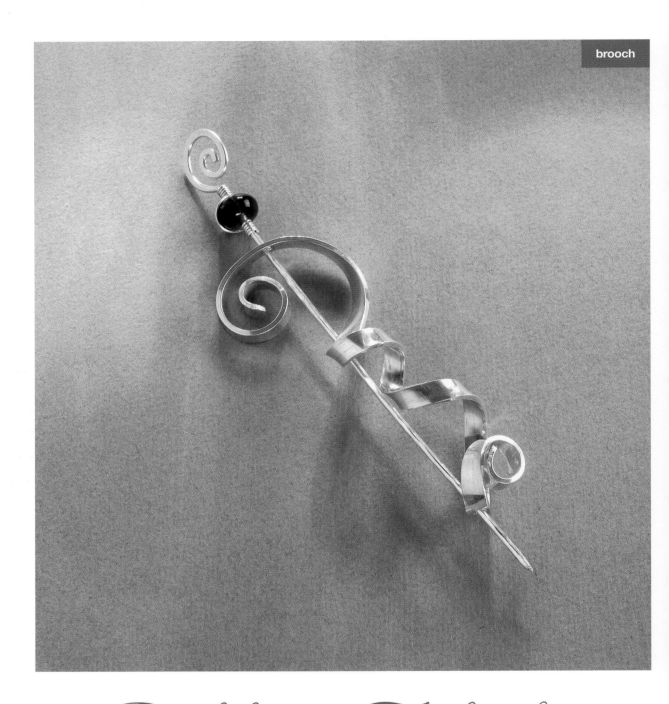

brooch

Ribbon Fibula

The fibula is a functional design used as a clothing fastener by many different civilizations, including the ancient Greeks and the Celts. Rectangular wire gives this version a playful personality and fresh appeal.

You'll need

Materials

7 in. (18 cm) 1 x 4 mm dead-soft rectangular sterling silver wire

5 in. (13 cm) 18-gauge dead-soft sterling silver wire

3 in. (76 mm) 24-gauge dead-soft sterling silver wire

6 x 8 mm bead

Tools and supplies

Chainnose pliers

Flatnose pliers

Roundnose pliers

Side cutters

File

Chasing hammer

Bench block

Screw-action punch

Sharpening stone (optional)

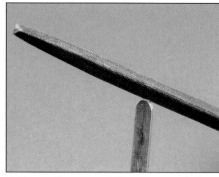

1 On one end, trim the corners off the rectangular wire.

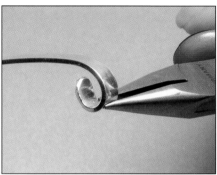

2 Use a flat metal file to round the ends of the wire.

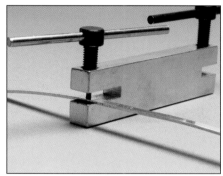

3 Use the small (silver) side of the screw-action punch to pierce two holes in the rectangular wire: the first about 2 in. (5 cm) from one end (for the top) and the second about 1 in. (2.5 cm) from the other end (the bottom).

4 For the top of the fibula, use chainnose pliers to begin making a spiral. Stop turning just before you get to the hole so the hole is unobstructed.

5 Continue shaping and spiraling the wire. To allow for the pin, the holes must align when you are finished shaping, and shapes must fall in front of the holes.

As you shape the rectangular wire, imagine an invisible vertical line representing the pin. You may find it helpful to sketch a shape on paper or use a practice wire first.

6 Test the alignment of the holes with a scrap wire and adjust them if necessary. Shape the lower spiral to fall in front of the pin.

7 To make the pin stem, make a spiral at the end of the 18-gauge wire. Insert the wire through both holes of the fibula from top to bottom and trim at an angle 1 in. past the lower hole. Remove the wire. Use a chasing hammer to create a slight texture on the spiral and the pin.

8 Sharpen the end of the pin with a sharpening stone or file.

9 String the bead onto the pin. Using 24-gauge wire, make five coils above the bead, a loose wrap over the bead, and another five coils below to secure the bead.

Rectangular wire makes a statement in a variety of jewelry components.

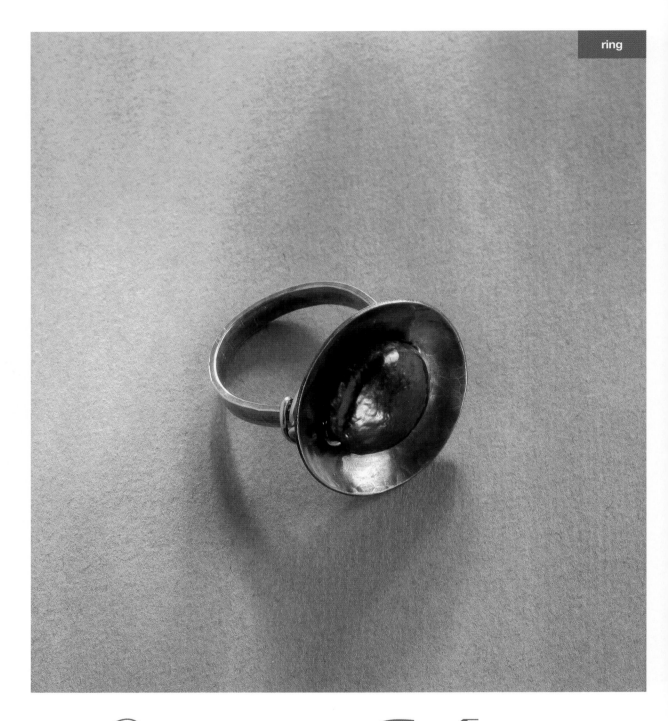

ring

Copper Moon

This domed disk frames the pearl, echoes its shape, and complements its texture. The different colors of metal harmonize for a striking result.

You'll need

Materials

6–8 in. (15–20 cm) 22-gauge dead-soft sterling silver wire

2½–3 in. (64–76 mm) 1 x 4 mm dead-soft rectangular sterling silver wire

1 in. (26 mm) diameter copper disk blank

12–14 mm coin pearl

Tools and supplies

Chainnose pliers

Flatnose pliers

Roundnose pliers

Side cutters

Screw-action punch

Hole-punching pliers

Bench block

Chasing hammer

Large metal file

Brass-head hammer

Metal dapping block and punches

Stepped ring mandrel

Paper

Pencil

Liver of sulfur (optional)

If you don't have access to a ring mandrel, measure your finger with a scrap of paper, then find a cylinder that has a similar circumference—try a thick marker or a utensil handle, for example.

1 To determine the length of rectangular wire needed, wrap a piece of paper around the desired size on the mandrel and mark it with a pencil.

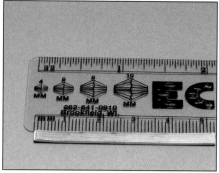

2 Measure the length, subtract 3 mm, and cut the rectangular wire to this length.

3 Use the chasing hammer to texture the rectangular wire.

4 Trim the corners of the wire on both ends and use the metal file to round the ends.

5 Punch a hole about 1–2 mm from each end.

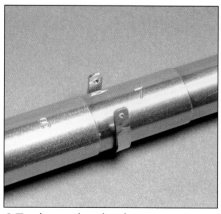

6 To shape the shank, curve the rectangular wire around the mandrel, using flatnose pliers to gently bend the wire if necessary.

7 Use flatnose pliers to bend the very ends of the shank slightly downward.

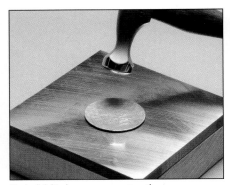

8 Add light texture to the copper disk with a chasing hammer.

9 To dome the disk, use a depression in the dapping block and a metal punch that are close to the size of the disk. Place the disk in the depression with the textured side up.

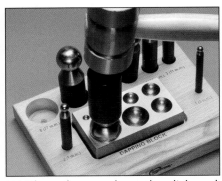

10 Place the punch on the disk and strike the punch with the brass-head hammer until the disk is domed.

11 Use hole-punching pliers to punch two holes in the domed disk. Make the distance between the holes slightly shorter than the length of the pearl.

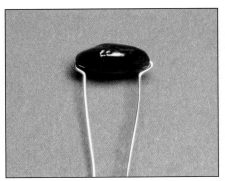

12 String the 22-gauge wire through the pearl and shape the wire around the sides of the pearl. Use chainnose pliers to make 90° bends as shown.

13 String the wire ends through the concave side of the disk, then through the holes in the ring shank.

14 Wrap both wire ends around the shank in the same direction.

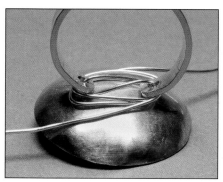

15 Wrap the wire three or four times around the shank.

16 Separate the wire ends and wrap each end around the side of the shank it is closest to two to three times. Make a small spiral on each side. Add patina with liver of sulfur if desired.

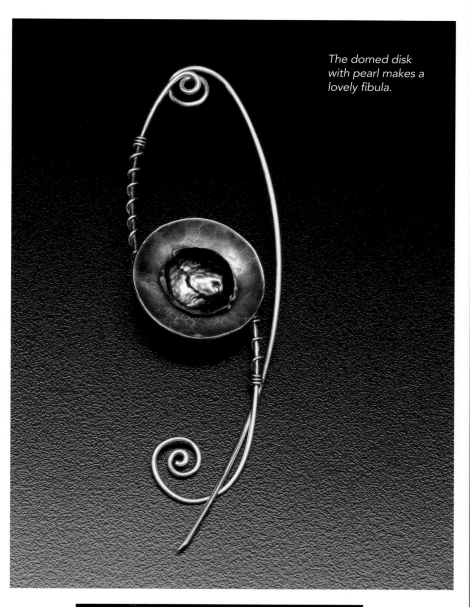

The domed disk with pearl makes a lovely fibula.

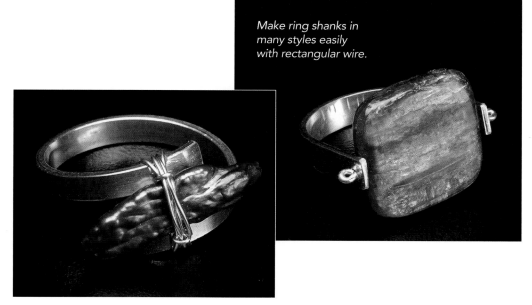

Make ring shanks in many styles easily with rectangular wire.

Ammonite Frame

Many of my organic designs are easily adapted to create structural pieces reminiscent of sea life. This one suggests an ammonite, a fossil of an extinct marine animal. The open center of this focal piece is a fitting frame for a sparkling rivoli.

You'll need

Materials

14 in. (36 cm) 18-gauge dead-soft sterling
   silver wire

8–10 ft. (2.4–3 m) 26-gauge gold-filled wire

Assorted size 11–15 seed beads, Charlottes,
   and 2–3 mm crystals

12 mm rivoli

16 in. (41 cm) sterling silver chain

6 6–7 mm gold-filled jump rings

3 8 mm sterling silver jump rings

Sterling silver hook clasp

Decorative headpin

Tools and supplies

Stepped forming pliers (5, 7, and 10 mm steps)

Chainnose pliers

Roundnose pliers

Flatnose pliers

Side cutters

Bench block

Chasing hammer

TO MAKE THE CENTERPIECE

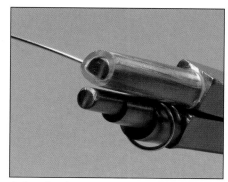

1 On the largest step of the forming pliers, make a loop at the end of the 18-gauge wire. Continue spiraling slightly past one full turn.

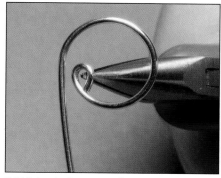

2 With chainnose pliers, make a small loop at the inner end of the wire.

You can substitute a cut stone or a CZ as the focal element for the centerpiece.

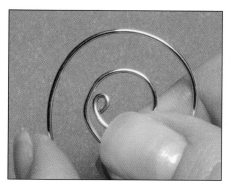

3 Continue making an open spiral using your fingers. Stop when you are satisfied with the size and shape of the spiral (mine is about 1½ in./38 mm across).

4 Lightly texture the spiral with the chasing hammer. Don't texture the last 1–2 in. (26–51 mm) of the wire.

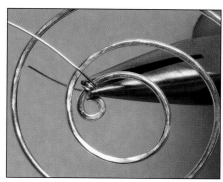

5 Cut a segment of gold-filled wire 1–2 ft. (30–61 cm) long. Leaving a short tail, attach the gold wire to the spiral by wrapping three to four times above the small loop.

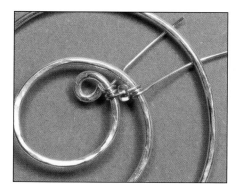

6 String a small bead on the working end of the gold wire and wrap the wire three to four times onto the next loop of the spiral. The wire should exit the back of the piece.

7 Pass the gold wire forward through the center of the spiral (not through the small loop). Wrap several times around the silver wire next to the previous wraps.

8 Continue adding beads to the piece as in steps 6 and 7, following the curve of the spiral and choosing amounts and sizes of beads that fit the gap between the center loop and adjacent (first) loop. Because of the spiral shape, you will smoothly transition so that you are beading the gap between the first and second loops, the second and third loops, and so on.

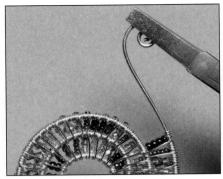

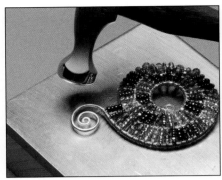

9 To add wire, end the working wire by wrapping several times around the silver wire, wrap a new wire in the same way, and continue beading. After stringing the last set of beads, trim and tuck the excess gold wire.

10 Trim the silver wire to approximately 2 in. (51 mm). Make a spiral as shown.

11 Lightly texture the spiral.

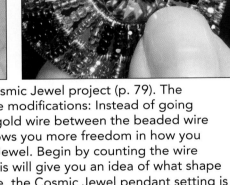

12 Using chainnose pliers, bend the small loop in the center of the piece to a 45° angle toward the back of the piece. Attach an 8-in. (20 cm) piece of gold wire to the back of the setting and string it through to the front on the outside of the center loop.

13 To set the rivoli, refer to the Cosmic Jewel project (p. 79). The technique is very similar, with these modifications: Instead of going through loops, you will string the gold wire between the beaded wire spokes. This spiral centerpiece allows you more freedom in how you anchor the rivoli than the Cosmic Jewel. Begin by counting the wire spokes around the center loop. This will give you an idea of what shape your setting could be. For example, the Cosmic Jewel pendant setting is a pentagon; this setting can be a square, a pentagon, or even a hexagon. Weave in and out of the wire spokes as desired. Go all the way around the rivoli to complete the setting.

TO MAKE THE NECKLACE

Attach gold-filled and silver jump rings to the spiral and to the opposite side of the centerpiece as shown. Attach lengths of chain to the jump rings. Finish by attaching a hook to one end with a jump ring and a wrapped-loop bead dangle to the other.

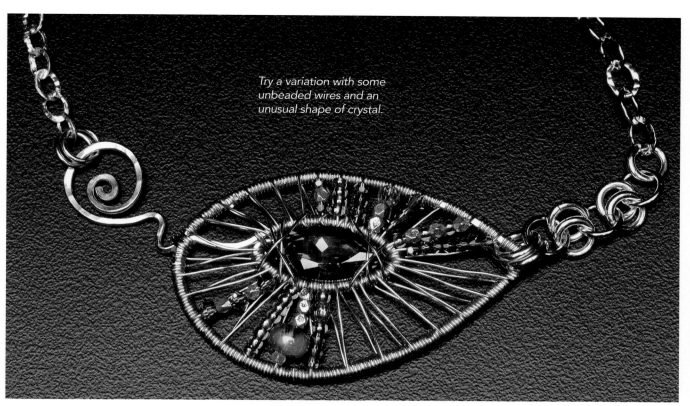

Try a variation with some unbeaded wires and an unusual shape of crystal.

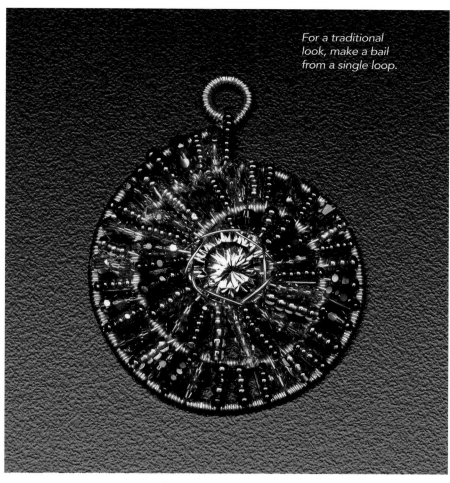

For a traditional look, make a bail from a single loop.

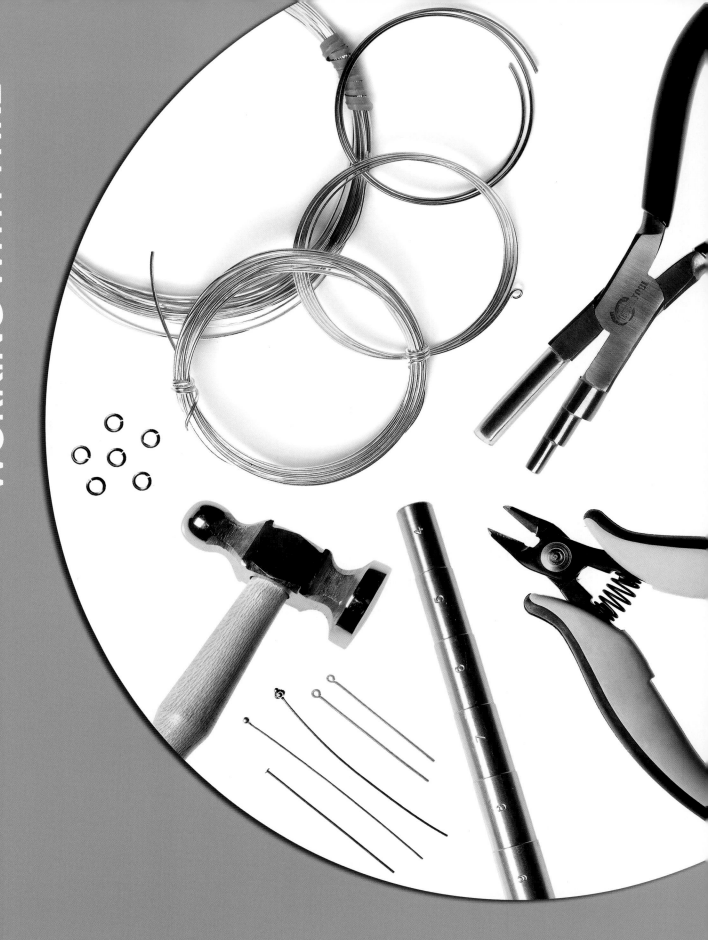

ABOUT WIRE

Wire is an essential material for many jewelry items, whether it's the foundation of the design or it plays a supporting role.

Sterling silver wire is used for many of the projects in this book. In some projects, you'll start with wire in the form of headpins and eyepins, which can be made of inexpensive **base metals** (often alloys, or mixes, of nonprecious metals such as copper or nickel) or **precious metals** such as sterling silver or gold.

If you like the color of gold in your designs, you'll most likely choose **gold-filled wire**. This high-quality metal is made by bonding an outside layer of gold to an interior base metal.

If you're new to shaping wire, you may want to practice the basic techniques shown on p. 107–108 with inexpensive copper or craft wire.

Wire comes in many different **gauges**, or thicknesses. The larger the number, the smaller the diameter of the wire. The projects in this book call for wire from fine 26-gauge to heavy 16-gauge.

Keep in mind that a bead's hole size will limit the diameter of wire that can be used with it; pearls typically have very small holes, for example, requiring a finer gauge of wire.

This system of gauging wire is used primarily in the United States. Other countries gauge wire by its metric measurement (see the gauge equivalents chart on the right).

Round wire is the most common wire shape and is used for most of the projects in this book. Other common shapes are half-round and square. Several projects call for rectangular wire that is 1 mm thick and 4 mm wide.

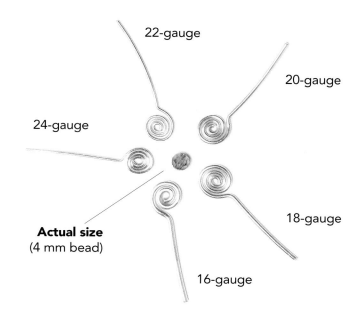

Actual size
(4 mm bead)

Temper refers to the hardness of the wire. Three tempers of wire are made: dead-soft, half-hard, and full-hard. They range from very pliable to very stiff. All wire hardens as you manipulate it; this is called **work-hardening**. Work-hardened pieces are stronger and they hold their shapes better than soft wire.

The projects in this book call for either **dead-soft** or **half-hard** wire. Dead-soft wire can be manipulated easily—even bent with your fingers. I always use dead-soft when I work with a thick gauge such as 18 or 16. I also use dead-soft in any gauge when I need to do a lot of coiling or wrapping; as it's worked, the wire hardens.

Half-hard wire has more resistance from the start and retains its shape well. If the shaping to be done is minimal and strength is important, use half-hard.

To work-harden wire after it is shaped, place it on a bench block and tap the wire with a metal hammer. If you tap very gently, you can harden the wire without changing its shape. Tapping with a rawhide or nylon mallet is another way to strengthen the wire without misshaping it. If you use a metal hammer with force, the wire will flatten as it hardens—which may be the effect you're after.

Wire gauge equivalents		
gauge	inches	mm
10	0.102	2.6
12	0.081	2.1
14	0.064	1.6
16	0.052	1.3
18	0.040	1.0
20	0.032	0.8
22	0.025	0.6
24	0.020	0.5
26	0.016	0.4
28	0.013	0.3

In the project instructions, most measurements are given in inches with a metric equivalent; bead sizes are given in metric, the worldwide standard for measuring beads.

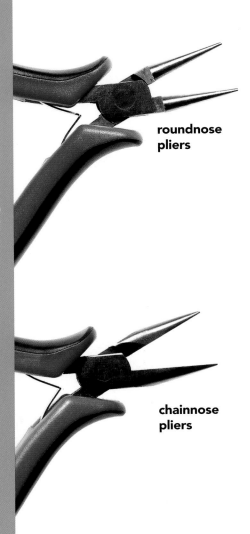

roundnose pliers

chainnose pliers

flatnose pliers

WIREWORKING TOOLS AND SUPPLIES

Everyone who works with wire needs a few basic tools in the beginning. Here I outline a **basic tool set** for wireworking and jewelry making; many tools are "must-haves" that are called for in the projects, and some are extras you may choose to add as you continue making jewelry. I also list some common findings and other supplies you'll want to have on hand.

Your pliers, in particular, will be in constant use. Purchase pliers designed specifically for making jewelry. The jaws of these pliers have a smooth, polished finish that won't mar your wire.

Ergonomically designed pliers and other tools have soft, comfortable grips that reduce stress on your hands. Often the handles are longer as well. Because I work with my pliers every day, I prefer using an ergonomic design.

Roundnose pliers are used to make loops and rounded curves and to start spirals. The nose of these pliers is cone-shaped, which allows you to make loops of various sizes. Working at the tip gives you a very tight loop; working at the base makes wider loops or curves.

The nose of my pliers is $^{13}/_{16}$ in. (21 mm) long. The point at which you form the loop on the nose determines the size of the loop created. Experience and practice will help you find the point that produces the size of loops that you like. To make consistently sized

loops, you can mark the pliers with permanent marker and always work at the same point.

Chainnose pliers have narrow, tapered jaws. They are used to bend and manipulate wire, and are especially useful for working in tight spaces. Two pairs can be used together for opening and closing jump rings, or use a pair of chainnose and a pair of flatnose pliers to do this.

Flatnose pliers, with wide, smooth jaws, are used to create broad bends in wire and for holding spiral components flat while shaping.

Stepped forming pliers are used to create uniformly sized rings, loops, or coils. One jaw has three steps for shaping three different sizes. The clear plastic guard on the other jaw lets you work without marring the

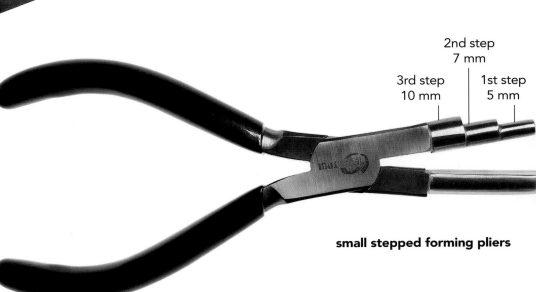

2nd step
7 mm

3rd step
10 mm

1st step
5 mm

small stepped forming pliers

wire. The projects call for the small size, which has 5, 7, and 10 mm steps; the large size is useful for shaping big clasps and loops. You may see other names for these pliers, including Wrap 'n' Tap pliers (the manufacturer's name for them) or stepped-roundnose pliers.

Although stepped forming pliers are handy, you can sometimes substitute a mandrel or bail-making pliers that match the diameter called for.

Crimping pliers are used with crimp beads to attach clasps or other findings to flexible beading wire.

Nylon-jaw pliers are used to straighten wire: Hold one end of the wire with chainnose pliers and pull the wire slowly through the non-marring nylon jaws to smooth out any bends or kinks. These are especially helpful when you are working with long pieces of wire.

Side cutters are the most common type of cutter used to cut wire for jewelry making. The term "side cutters" describes any cutters with blades that are parallel to the handles. Within the side cutters category, you can choose the type of blades you prefer. You'll find trade-offs between blade durability, cutting power, and the shapes left

on the cut wire ends. **Bevel cutters** are durable, economical, and can cut very thick wire. They leave pronounced V shapes on the wire ends, so if your design requires flat ends, you'll need to file them. On the other end of the cutting spectrum are **super-flush cutters**, which leave flat wire ends. These cutters are best reserved for wire that's thinner than 18-gauge.

A good choice in side cutters is **multipurpose flush cutters**, which fall between bevel cutters and super-flush cutters in durability and cut. I use my flush cutters to cut precious-metal wire as well as flexible beading wire. If you prefer to use super-flush cutters, which aren't designed for cutting beading wire, or you simply want to prolong the life of your primary cutters, purchase a second pair of inexpensive bevel cutters and use them for cutting only beading wire.

Never use the side cutters you use for precious-metal wire to cut steel wire such as memory wire.

Tool Magic is very helpful for beginning wireworkers. Dip the jaws of any pliers in this liquid and let it dry into a rubbery coating to help prevent damage to wire.

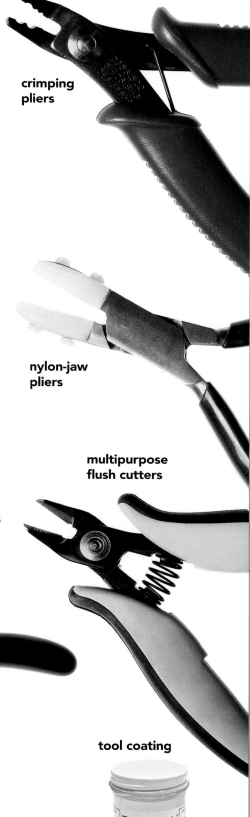

crimping pliers

nylon-jaw pliers

multipurpose flush cutters

tool coating

1st step
13 mm

2nd step
16 mm

3rd step
20 mm

large stepped forming pliers

pin vise

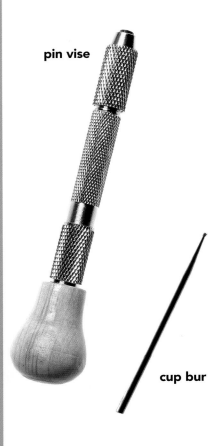

cup bur

bench block

A **pin vise** is a hand tool with a collet (or chuck) at one end. By tightening the collet around the end of a wire or wires, I can use it to twist square wire and to twist multiple wires together. The pin vise can also hold other bits such as drill bits, bead reamers, or cup burs.

A **cup bur** is used to round and smooth the ends of wire, and is especially helpful when making earring wires. The cup holds tiny file teeth that smooth the wire end as you turn the tool clockwise.

A **bench block** is a polished steel surface used for flattening, straightening, or hardening wire. A 2-in. (51 mm) square block is large enough for making most wire jewelry projects. Blocks may be solid steel or wood with a steel surface.

A **chasing hammer** has one large, very slightly convex face, used for flattening and hardening. The other end is ball shaped and is used for texturing. For most wire jewelry projects, a hammer with a 1-in. (26 mm) face will work well.

A **sharpening stone** is used to file a wire end to a smooth point. You'll use this tool when you create pins, such as the brooch on p. 88.

Files come in a variety of shapes and sizes. A single metal file with at least one flat side will be useful. Or choose a versatile set of **mini files** in a variety of profiles, including flat, round, and half-round.

Although you can use nearly any kind of cylinder as a mandrel, tools are made specifically for this purpose. A **stepped ring mandrel** is a cone-shaped tool that has steps marked with a range of ring sizes. For working with wire, use a steel ring mandrel.

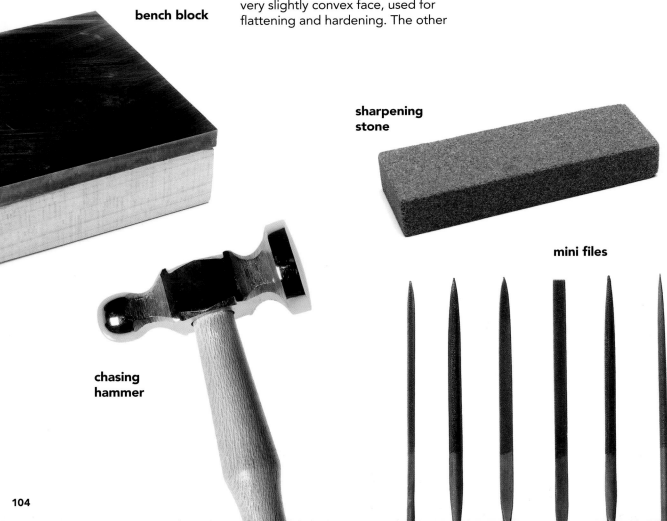

sharpening stone

mini files

chasing hammer

Keep a **ruler** on your work surface; you'll need it for many wireworking projects. I like a short, see-through ruler with both metric, the standard for measuring beads, and Imperial (inch) markings that are commonly used in the U.S.

If you like to antique your wirework with liver of sulfur solution, keep some metal **tweezers** handy. Use them to place objects into and remove them from the solution.

Jump rings are available in many diameters and gauges. If a project calls for jump rings, assume that they are open (not soldered closed).

From the tiniest link to the largest, **chain** adds movement to jewelry designs. Chain can also be used to create a necklace extender: Pair chain with a hook, and you have an adjustable necklace. Jewelry supply stores will cut chain off large spools, so you can usually buy just the length needed for a project.

The most common **earwire** style, and the easiest to make by hand, is the French hook. Many types, such as the secure lever-back style, are available ready-made.

Headpins are short lengths of wire with a stopper at the bottom to hold beads in place. Purchased headpins may have a simple stopper that looks like a nail head, or they may have a decorative detail. **Eyepins** have a ready-made loop at one end. Common gauges of headpins and eyepins are 24- and 22-gauge.

I usually use 24-gauge or finer for making wrapped loops and 22-gauge or thicker for making basic loops. A 2-in. (51 mm) pin will give you extra length to work with; in many cases, a 1½-in. (38 mm) pin will be long enough. It's a good idea to keep a supply of headpins and eyepins in various sizes and finishes on hand.

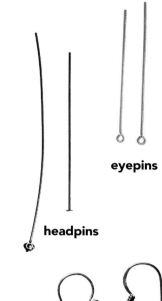

eyepins

headpins

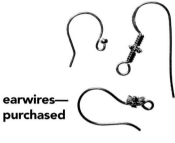

earwires—purchased

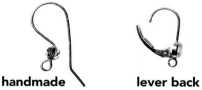

handmade

lever back

stepped ring mandrel

jump rings

tweezers

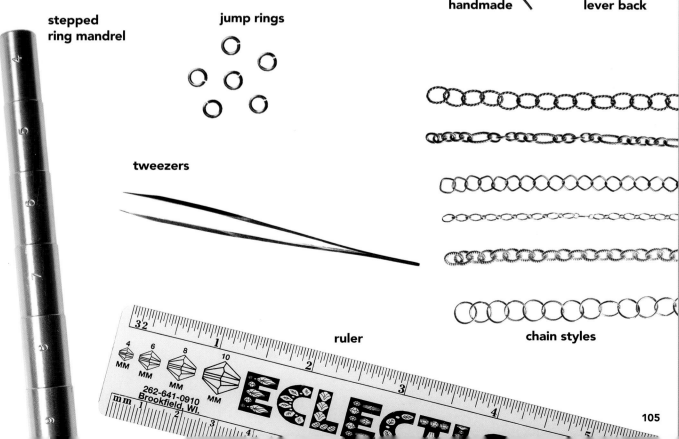

ruler

chain styles

262-641-0910
Brookfield, WI.

ECLECTI

hook clasps

lobster-claw clasp

toggle set

crimp tubes

crimp end

Clasps are a functional component and should be considered as a design element that enhances or complements a jewelry piece. There are a variety of clasps available, such as toggle clasps, hooks, lobster claws, and many others. In addition, you can create your own out of wire.

Crimps are small metal tubes that connect clasps and other findings to flexible beading wire. Use crimping pliers to tighten and fold the crimp around the beading wire.

Crimp ends are designed to finish cords such as leather or cotton; insert the cord and squeeze the tube's center with chainnose pliers to secure. (You can add a dab of E6000 or similar glue for extra security.)

Flexible beading wire is made of strands of stainless steel wire encased in a nylon coating. Although no projects in this book call for beading wire, you'll find it

indispensable if you enjoy making beaded jewelry. There are different sizes available; I use .010–.019 mm most often for bead stringing. Flexible beading wire does not knot well, so use crimps to finish the ends and attach them to clasp components.

Cones are used to gather and conceal multiple strands or chains. They are usually made of metal.

Liver of sulfur is a chemical used to add a patina, or antique look, to metal. Liver of sulfur can be purchased as dry chunks or in liquid or gel form. I prefer the dry form because it's economical; I use a small chunk dissolved in warm water to make what I need each time.

Small **polishing pads** work well for removing patina from the high points of metal or wire.

cones

liver of sulfur chunks

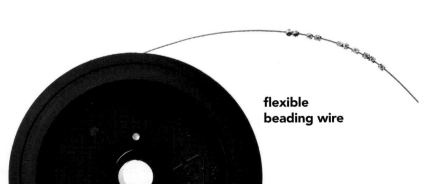

flexible beading wire

polishing pads

WIREWORKING TECHNIQUES

Working from the wire coil

If you work with wire often, as I do, you'll find it most economical as well as a real time-saver to work directly from the wire coil. If you cut small lengths for each step, you'll need to trim the excess, thus accumulating a lot of short bits of wasted wire. You can save time by eliminating several cutting and trimming steps.

Unless the project instructions specify a cut length for a step, assume you are working from the wire coil. If you are making basic or wrapped loops, place the bead on the wire first. If you forget and make one loop before you string the bead, you can string the bead on the other wire end.

I begin with no more than 10 ft. (3 m) of coiled wire. Heavier-gauge wire is often sold in shorter coils; for example, my 18-gauge wire starts out as a 5-ft. (1.5 m) coil.

Some instructions call for forming loops over beads on headpins or eyepins. The process for making basic and wrapped loops is very similar whether you are using a pin or working from the wire coil.

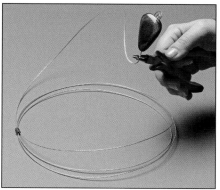

Working from the wire coil is more efficient than cutting short lengths of wire for each step.

Making a basic loop above a bead

1 String a bead on a headpin or the wire coil. Make a right-angle bend over the bead.

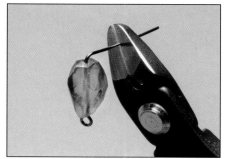

2 Trim the wire to ⅜ in. (1 cm).

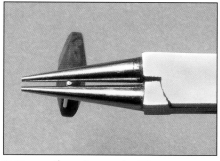

3 Grasp the wire end with roundnose pliers. Make sure the end is flush with the jaws.

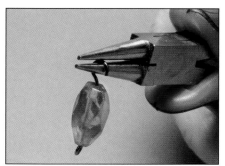

4 Roll the wire around the jaw in the opposite direction of the bend to form a circle.

5 If necessary, reposition the pliers in the loop to continue rolling into a full circle. You may attach another component before closing the loop completely.

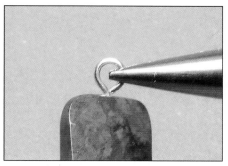

6 Use chainnose pliers to close the loop completely.

To make loops on both sides of the bead, work from the coil and repeat the process on the opposite side.

Making a wrapped loop

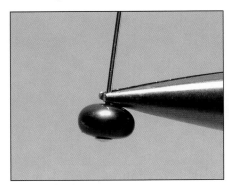

Begin the loop:
1 String a bead on a headpin or the wire coil. Grasp the wire with the tip of the chainnose pliers just above the bead if on a headpin and 1¼ in./32 mm from the end if on the wire coil.

2 Use your fingers to bend the wire over the pliers at a 90° angle.

3 Place the roundnose pliers just past the bend. Wrap the wire over the top jaw as far as it will go. Rotate the pliers in the loop and continue wrapping until you have a full circle.

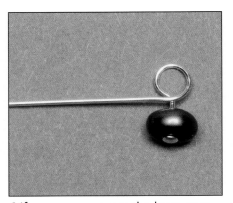

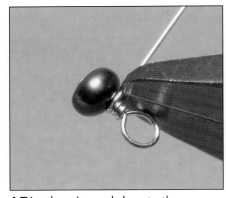

4 If necessary, center the loop over the bead by turning the pliers slightly while holding the bead. When the loop is centered, the wire should cross itself at a 90° angle. At this point, the loop is open and you can connect it to another component.

Finish the loop:
5 Holding the loop with chainnose pliers, use your fingers or a second set of pliers to wrap the wire into the gap between the loop and the bead. Make 2–3 wraps.

6 Trim the wire end close to the wraps.

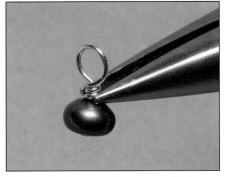

I am right-handed, and the photos show the actions as I do them. Most left-handers will need to use a mirror-image motion.

7 Use chainnose pliers to tuck the wire end tightly between the wraps and the bead.

Making spirals

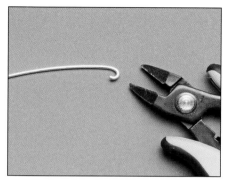

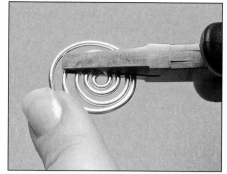

1 Make a loop at the end of the wire with roundnose pliers; trim the tip of the loop if it is not curved.

2 Continue shaping the wire to form a second loop around the first.

3 Grasp the spiral with flatnose pliers and turn the spiral while guiding the wire with your finger. Loosen the grip, regrip the spiral, and continue shaping until the spiral is the desired size.

Hammering

Use the smooth, slightly convex face of the **chasing hammer** to flatten and harden your wirework. Use the rounded end to add texture. Use a **texture hammer** to add overall pattern to the surface of metal or wire.

Work on a bench block placed on a solid, sturdy work surface. For the best control of your hammer, grasp it at its base.

Pay careful attention so you can control the points on the wire that become flattened or textured.

To flatten wire: With careful aim, you can control how wide the wire gets and at which points it spreads.

To add texture: The rounded end will add small divots of texture to the wire. Tap the piece while moving around the surface of the wire.

Smoothing wire ends

This technique is especially handy for finishing the ends of earwires so they are smooth and comfortable to wear.

Place the wire end in the cup bur and turn the tool in short rotations.

Check with your fingertip to feel if the end of the wire is smooth. Repeat if necessary.

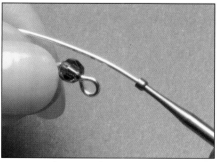

Rotate the cup bur in one direction only rather than using a back-and-forth motion.

Using liver of sulfur

Dip silver in liver-of-sulfur solution to add a beautiful sheen, or patina, in a progression of colors starting with amber and ranging through magenta, blue, dark gray, and black.

Use liver of sulfur with proper ventilation; avoid breathing the fumes and avoid skin contact. Work near running water or keep a container of cool water handy to stop the action of the solution. After drying the piece, use a small polishing pad to highlight the raised areas, leaving the patina in the recesses for an antique look.

To use: In a small plastic container dedicated to use with liver of sulfur, dissolve a chunk in about a cup of warm water. The water will turn light yellow, and you will smell the strong odor of sulfur (like rotten eggs).

Immerse your silver piece (it's fine to drop it in the solution). When you see a patina color you like, remove the piece with tweezers, rinse in cool water, and dry. Repeat the process to darken the patina if desired.

Making Z bends in wire

Short bends add decorative detail and tighten tension on wires. Grasp the wire with chainnose pliers and rotate to form a small Z shape.

Using stepped forming pliers

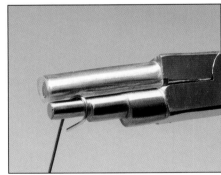

The three steps on these pliers help you make large, consistently sized curves, rings, coils, or loops. Try wrapping wire at each step to see the results.

Opening jump rings and basic loops

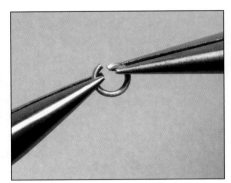

To open: Using two sets of pliers, grasp one end of the ring in the tip of each pliers. Move one set of pliers toward you and one away to open the ring slightly. **To close:** Reverse the motion. Use the same method to open a basic loop, add components, and close the loop.

About the Author

Irina Miech has been involved in the world of jewelry making for more than 20 years. She owns the retail bead store Eclectica, and she offers instruction in wirework, beading, and metal clay techniques through her Bead Studio.

This is Irina's sixth book and a follow-up to her first wirework book, *Beautiful Wire Jewelry for Beaders*. She has authored four books of metal clay jewelry projects and also contributes projects to *Bead&Button*, *BeadStyle*, *Art Jewelry*, and other publications.

Irina is a graduate of the University of Wisconsin–Milwaukee. She lives with her husband and sons in southeastern Wisconsin.

ACKNOWLEDGMENTS

I would like to thank my husband, Tony Miech, for his unwavering support of my work; Lauren Walsh for her writing advice; and my sons, Zachary and David, for their encouragement and love. I thank my editor, Mary Wohlgemuth, and the rest of the Kalmbach staff for their invaluable assistance. Thanks also to my wonderful store staff members for all of their enthusiastic help and continual support.

SOURCES

All of the wire, beads, and findings used in my projects came from Eclectica, my retail bead store in Wisconsin. I hope you'll support your local bead and craft stores as you select your project supplies.

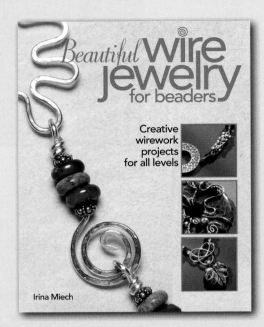

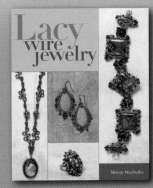
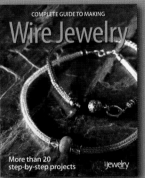
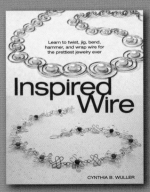